The 5-Ingredient
Keto Diet Cookbook
for Beginners

**140 Easy 30 Minute Low Carb High Fat Recipes
for Effective Weight Loss and Metabolism-boosting
with 30 - Day Meal Plan | Full Color Edition**

Mia Norman

Table of Contents:

Table of Contents:

Introduction

Welcome to The 5-Ingredient Keto Cookbook for Beginners! Whether you're just starting your keto journey or looking for simple, delicious recipes to make your life easier, this book is your guide. Focusing on recipes with just five ingredients, we've taken the guesswork out of meal prep and created a resource perfect for busy schedules, tight budgets, and anyone who loves good food without the fuss.

The ketogenic diet doesn't have to be complicated. With its emphasis on high-fat ingredients, moderate protein, and low carbs, keto isn't just a diet — it's a lifestyle that can help you lose weight, increase your energy, and improve your overall health. However, thinking about complicated recipes or hard-to-find ingredients often stops people in their tracks. That's where this cookbook shines: I've combined keto principles with the simplicity of five-ingredient cooking to make your transition smooth and your meals filling.

You'll find recipes ranging from quick breakfasts to hearty meat dishes, filling snacks, and even decadent desserts. Each recipe is designed to pack maximum flavor with minimal effort, making it easier than ever to stay on track with your health goals.

Why 5 Ingredients?

Life is busy, and cooking should be enjoyable—not a chore. By limiting recipes to just five key ingredients, we make cooking approachable, affordable, and time-saving. Plus, these recipes use everyday keto-friendly staples, so you'll spend less time shopping and more time enjoying delicious meals with your family and friends. Each recipe is crafted to bring maximum flavor with minimal effort, making it easier than ever to stay on track with your health goals.

Thank you for choosing this book and taking the first step toward a healthier, more vibrant life. Whether you're new to keto or a seasoned pro, trust in these recipes means the world to us. We hope this cookbook inspires you to create love meals while staying true to your health goals.

Let's Get Cooking!

Ready to dive in? Turn the page and start exploring the wonderful world of five-ingredient keto recipes. It's time to simplify your cooking, delight your taste buds, and take the stress out of meal planning. You've got this—and we're thrilled to be part of your journey.

Here's to your success: one delicious meal at a time!

Happy cooking,

Mia Norman

CHAPTER 1: Getting Started with Keto

What is the Keto Diet?

The ketogenic (keto) diet is a low-carbohydrate, high-fat diet that encourages your body to enter a metabolic state called ketosis. In ketosis, your body shifts from burning carbohydrates for energy to burning fat, which is converted into ketones in the liver. The keto diet is renowned for its potential to aid in weight loss, improve mental clarity, and stabilize blood sugar levels. It transforms your metabolism and promotes fat burning by drastically reducing carbohydrate intake and replacing it with fat.

A Brief Explanation of Keto Principles:

The keto diet's core revolves around three key macronutrients: fats, proteins, and carbohydrates. The diet emphasizes high-fat consumption, moderate protein intake, and very low carbohydrate levels, typically less than 50 grams daily. By minimizing carbs, the body depletes its glycogen stores and uses fat as its primary energy source. This process leads to the production of ketones, which fuel the body and brain efficiently. Adherence to these macronutrient ratios is essential for achieving and maintaining ketosis.

Benefits of Following a Keto Lifestyle:

The keto lifestyle offers numerous advantages beyond weight loss:

- **Enhanced Fat Burning:** The keto diet supports efficient fat burning by utilizing fat as the primary fuel source.
- **Improved Mental Clarity and Focus:** Ketones provide a stable and clean energy source for the brain, reducing brain fog and enhancing cognitive function.
- **Blood Sugar Stabilization:** Lower carbohydrate intake helps regulate blood sugar levels, benefitting those with insulin resistance or type 2 diabetes.
- **Increased Energy:** With fewer blood sugar spikes and crashes, keto followers often experience more sustained energy throughout the day.
- **Appetite Control:** The high-fat content of keto meals promotes satiety, reducing hunger and curbing cravings.
- **Potential Health Benefits:** Research suggests the keto diet may help reduce inflammation, improve cholesterol levels, and support neurological health.

Why 5 Ingredients?

Simplifying your keto meals with only five ingredients ensures that cooking is quick, efficient, and accessible for beginners and busy individuals. Fewer ingredients mean:

- **Time-Saving:** Reduced prep and cooking time make it easier to stick to your diet.
- **Effortless Shopping:** Shorter shopping lists eliminate the overwhelming need to purchase numerous items.
- **Cost-Effectiveness:** Fewer ingredients can lower grocery bills without sacrificing flavor or nutrition.
- **Consistency:** A simplified approach makes keto cooking less daunting, increasing your chances of long-term success.

Getting Started with Keto

Understanding Macros:

Macronutrients, or macros, are the building blocks of the keto diet. Understanding their roles is essential for achieving ketosis:

✓ Fats: Your primary energy source, making up 70-80% of your daily intake. Examples include avocados, butter, and olive oil.

✓ Proteins: Required for muscle repair and overall health, making up 20-25% of your intake. Opt for lean cuts of meat, fish, and eggs.

✓ Carbohydrates: Limited to 5-10% of your intake, focusing on non-starchy vegetables and low-carb fruits.

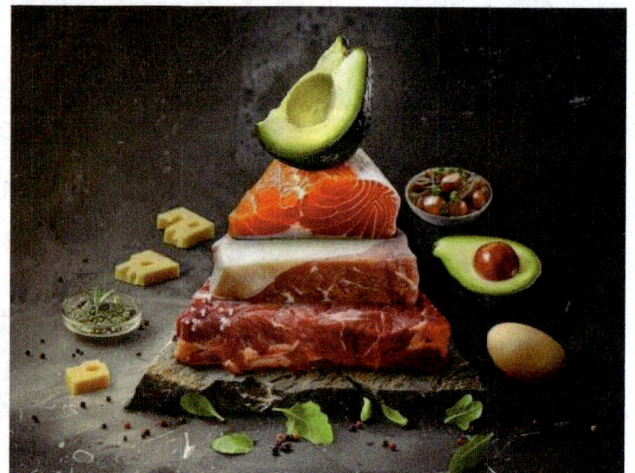

Understanding the Keto Flu: Symptoms and Prevention

Transitioning to the ketogenic diet can be an exciting step toward achieving better health, weight loss, and improved energy. However, for some beginners, the shift to a high-fat, low-carb lifestyle can come with an unexpected side effect known as the "keto flu." This temporary phase is your body's response to adapting to ketosis, the metabolic state where fat becomes your primary fuel source instead of carbohydrates. Understanding keto flu symptoms and how to minimize its effects can make your keto journey smoother and more enjoyable.

What is the Keto Flu?

The keto flu is not an actual illness but a collection of symptoms that occur as your body adjusts to drastically reduced carbohydrate intake. When carbs are reduced, your body depletes glycogen stores and relies on fat for fuel. This metabolic shift can create temporary imbalances in electrolytes and hormones, leading to unpleasant side effects.

Symptoms of the Keto Flu:

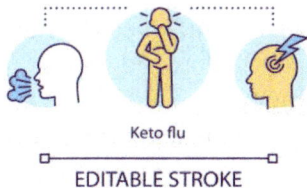

Keto flu

EDITABLE STROKE

The symptoms of keto flu can vary from person to person but often include:

- **Fatigue:** Feeling unusually tired or sluggish.
- **Headache:** Persistent or mild headaches, often linked to dehydration.
- **Nausea:** A queasy stomach or lack of appetite.
- **Dizziness:** Lightheadedness due to electrolyte imbalances.
- **Irritability:** Mood swings or feeling "grumpy."
- **Brain fog:** Difficulty concentrating or experiencing mental clarity.
- **Muscle cramps:** Aching or cramping muscles caused by low potassium or magnesium levels.
- **Constipation or diarrhea:** Digestive discomfort as our body adjusts to new dietary patterns.

These symptoms typically last a few days to a week as your body adapts to its new energy source.

How to Minimize the Keto Flu:

The good news is that the keto flu is temporary and manageable. Here are some strategies to reduce its impact:

1. Stay Hydrated

Dehydration is a common cause of keto flu symptoms. As glycogen stores deplete, water is released, leading to increased urination. Drink plenty of water throughout the day to maintain hydration.

2. Replenish Electrolytes

Electrolyte imbalances can cause symptoms like dizziness and muscle cramps. Ensure you get adequate amounts of sodium, potassium, and magnesium by:
- Adding a pinch of salt to your water or meals.
- Incorporating keto-friendly foods rich in these minerals, such as avocados, leafy greens, and bone broth.
- Considering electrolyte supplements if needed.

3. Gradually Reduce Carbs

Instead of jumping into a strict keto diet overnight, gradually decrease your carbohydrate intake over a week or two. This gives your body time to adjust and reduces the severity of keto flu symptoms.

4. Prioritize Healthy Fats

Eating enough high-quality fats ensures your body has sufficient energy while adapting to ketosis. Include fats like olive oil, coconut oil, butter, and fatty cuts of meat in your diet.

5. Get Plenty of Sleep

Quality sleep is essential for recovery and adaptation. Aim for 7-8 hours of uninterrupted sleep each night to support your body during the transition.

6. Stay Active, But Don't Overdo It

Light exercise like walking or yoga can help boost energy and reduce symptoms. Avoid intense workouts during the first week of transitioning to keto, as your body may not have fully adapted to burning fat for fuel.

Foods to Eat and Avoid for Optimal Results:

The ketogenic diet has gained popularity for its potential to promote weight loss, enhance energy levels, and improve overall health. Central to its success is making informed dietary choices, which involves knowing what foods to embrace and which to avoid. This guide provides a detailed breakdown of Keto-friendly foods, their benefits, and tips for navigating the diet successfully.

Foods to Eat on the Keto Diet

The Keto diet emphasizes high-fat, moderate-protein, and low-carbohydrate foods. These choices help shift your body into ketosis, where fat becomes the primary fuel source instead of carbohydrates. Here are the key categories of Keto-friendly foods:

1.Healthy Fats and Oils:

Examples: Olive oil, coconut oil, avocado oil, butter, ghee, and lard.
Why Recommended: Healthy fats provide the most calories in the keto diet. They support brain health, hormone production, and sustained energy.
Tips:
- Use avocado oil for high-heat cooking and olive oil for salad dressings.
- Incorporate fats like butter or ghee into sautéed vegetables for added richness.

2.Low-Carb Vegetables:

Examples: Spinach, kale, broccoli, cauliflower, zucchini, asparagus, and bell peppers.
Why Recommended: These vegetables are low in carbohydrates and high in fiber, vitamins, and minerals, supporting digestion and overall health.
Tips:
- Roast cauliflower as a rice substitute or spiralize zucchini for noodles.
- Incorporate leafy greens into smoothies or salads for extra nutrients.

3.Proteins:

Examples: Grass-fed beef, poultry, eggs, fatty fish (e.g., salmon, mackerel), and pork.
Why Recommended: Protein supports muscle maintenance, immunity, and satiety without disrupting ketosis when consumed in moderation.
Tips:
- Choose fatty cuts of meat like ribeye or pork belly for additional fat content.
- Hard-boil eggs for convenient, portable as a dairy alternative.

4.Dairy Products:

Examples: Cheese, cream, Greek yogurt (unsweetened), and butter.
Why Recommended: Full-fat dairy products are rich in fats and flavor, making them excellent additions to meals and snacks.
Tips:
- Use cream to create rich sauces or add to coffee for a creamy texture.
- Top dishes with shredded cheese for an indulgent finish.

5.Nuts and Seeds:

Examples: Almonds, walnuts, macadamia nuts, chia seeds, and flaxseeds.
Why Recommended: Nuts and seeds provide healthy fats, protein, and fiber while adding crunch and variety to meals.
Tips:
- Limit portion sizes to avoid excess carbs.
- Use almond flour or coconut flour as Keto-friendly baking alternatives.

6.Low-Sugar Fruits:

Examples: Berries (strawberries, raspberries, blackberries), avocados, and olives.
Why Recommended: These fruits are low in sugar but high in antioxidants, vitamins, and healthy fats.
Tips:
- Add a handful of berries to Greek yogurt for a sweet treat.
- Incorporate avocado into smoothies or as a base for guacamole.

7.Beverages:

Examples: Water, herbal teas, coffee, and bone broth.
Why Recommended: Staying hydrated is critical for keto; these options support hydration without added sugars.
Tips:
- Flavor water with lemon slices or cucumber.
- Choose unsweetened almond or coconut milk as a dairy alternative.

Foods to Avoid on the Keto Diet:

To maintain ketosis, certain foods need to be avoided or strictly limited. These foods can spike blood sugar levels, disrupt ketosis, and hinder progress.

1. High-Carb Foods

- **Examples**: Bread, pasta, rice, cereals, and starchy vegetables (potatoes, corn, peas).
- **Why Restricted**: High-carb foods elevate blood sugar levels, which prevents the body from using fat as its primary energy source.
- **Overcoming Challenges**:
  - Substitute with cauliflower rice, zucchini noodles, or almond flour bread.

2. Sugary Foods and Drinks

- **Examples**: Candy, sodas, fruit juices, cakes, and cookies.
- **Why Restricted**: Sugar provides empty calories and can cause blood sugar spikes.
- **Overcoming Challenges**:
  - Opt for Keto-friendly sweeteners like stevia or erythritol.
  - Prepare homemade Keto desserts using almond or coconut flour.

3. Grains and Grain-Based Foods

- **Examples**: Wheat, oats, barley, and corn.
- **Why Restricted**: Grains are high in carbs and lack the fat required for Keto.
- **Overcoming Challenges**:
  - Use almond or coconut flour for baking and cooking.

4. Legumes

- **Examples**: Lentils, chickpeas, black beans, and peanuts.
- **Why Restricted**: Legumes are high in carbohydrates and can disrupt ketosis.
- **Overcoming Challenges**:
  - Replace legumes with Keto-friendly nuts or seeds for added texture and protein.

5. Processed Foods

- **Examples**: Chips, crackers, processed meats (with added sugars), and frozen meals.
- **Why Restricted**: These foods often contain hidden carbs, unhealthy fats, and preservatives.
- **Overcoming Challenges**:
  - Prepare meals in advance to avoid relying on processed options.

How to Read Food Labels on the Keto Diet:

Being mindful of ingredients is crucial for staying in ketosis. Here's what to look for:

- ✓ **Net Carbs**: Subtract fiber and sugar alcohols from total carbohydrates to calculate net carbs.
- ✓ **Hidden Sugars**: Watch for ingredients like maltodextrin, dextrose, and syrups.
- ✓ **Fats and Proteins**: Opt for foods with higher fat content and moderate protein levels.
- ✓ **Ingredients List**: Shorter lists with recognizable ingredients are preferable.

Empowering Your Keto Journey

Transitioning to a Keto lifestyle may feel overwhelming at first, but with the right knowledge and tools, it can be an enjoyable and rewarding experience. Experiment with the recommended foods to discover flavors and recipes that excite you. Remember, small changes lead to significant progress. With confidence and consistency, you can achieve your health and dietary goals while savoring delicious and satisfying meals.

Going Keto in Ten Steps:

Adopting the ketogenic diet can seem daunting at first, but breaking it down into manageable steps can make the transition smooth and sustainable. Follow these ten simple steps to begin your keto journey successfully:

Step 1: Understand the Basics of Keto

The ketogenic diet is a high-fat, moderate-protein, and low-carbohydrate eating plan designed to put your body into a state of ketosis. In ketosis, your body burns fat for energy instead of carbohydrates. This shift can aid in weight loss, improve mental clarity, and boost energy levels. Familiarize yourself with the macronutrient breakdown: typically 70-80% fats, 20-25% protein, and 5-10% carbohydrates.

Step 2: Educate Yourself on Keto-Friendly Foods

Stock your kitchen with keto-friendly staples. Focus on healthy fats like avocado, olive oil, and butter; proteins such as chicken, beef, fish, and eggs; and low-carb vegetables like spinach, zucchini, and cauliflower. Avoid high-carb foods like bread, pasta, sugary snacks, and starchy vegetables.

Step 3: Plan Your Meals

Meal planning is crucial for staying on track. Start with simple recipes using five ingredients or fewer to ease into the diet. Having a plan helps prevent impulsive food choices that could derail your progress.

Step 4: Track Your Macros

Use a macro-tracking app to ensure you stay within the keto guidelines. Record your daily intake of fats, proteins, and carbohydrates. This will help you maintain the correct balance and avoid exceeding your carb limit.

Step 5: Prepare for Keto Flu

As your body transitions into ketosis, you may experience flu-like symptoms, known as the "keto flu." These symptoms—fatigue, headaches, and irritability—are temporary. Stay hydrated, increase your electrolyte intake (through foods like spinach, nuts, and avocados), and rest as needed.

Step 6: Hydrate and Replenish Electrolytes

Water is essential in the keto diet. Aim to drink at least eight glasses a day to stay hydrated. Additionally, include sodium, potassium, and magnesium-rich foods in your meals to maintain electrolyte balance.

Step 7: Start Slow

Ease into keto gradually. Begin by reducing your carbohydrate intake over a few days instead of cutting carbs drastically all at once. This approach can make the adjustment more manageable and minimize side effects.

Step 8: Keep Snacks Simple

Prepare keto-friendly snacks to prevent hunger and maintain energy levels. Options like cheese sticks, hard-boiled eggs, or a handful of nuts can keep you satisfied between meals.

Step 9: Monitor Your Progress

Regularly check your weight, energy levels, and overall mood. Some people also use keto testing strips to measure their ketone levels. This feedback can motivate you to stay consistent and make adjustments if necessary.

Step 10: Stay Consistent and Flexible

Consistency is key to seeing results on the ketogenic diet. However, allow yourself flexibility and patience as you adapt. Remember, this is a lifestyle change, not a short-term fix. Focus on long-term goals and celebrate small victories along the way.

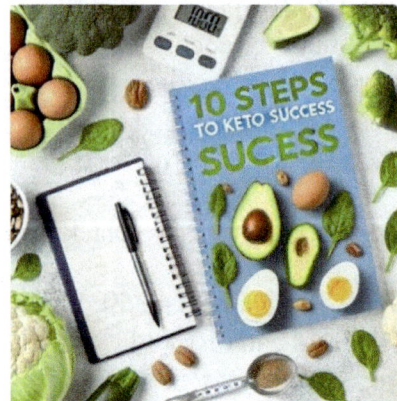

These ten steps will set you up for success in your keto journey. Remember, simplicity is at the heart of the ketogenic diet—even with just five ingredients, you can create delicious and satisfying meals while transforming your health.

1.Keto Scrambled Eggs with Cream Cheese

Serves: 2 | Prep: 3 minutes | Cook : 5 minutes

Ingredients:

- 4 medium eggs
- 50g full-fat cream cheese
- 1 tablespoon butter
- ¼ teaspoon salt
- ¼ teaspoon black pepper

Instructions:

1.In a medium bowl, whisk the eggs with salt and black pepper until well combined.
2.Heat the butter in a non-stick frying pan over medium-low heat.
3.Once melted, pour in the eggs and gently stir with a spatula for about 2-3 minutes until they start to set.
4.Add the cream cheese in small dollops and continue to cook, folding the cream cheese into the eggs until creamy and fully incorporated.
5.Remove from the heat just before the eggs are fully set to keep them soft and creamy. Serve warm.

Chef's Tip: *Stirring constantly and cooking over low heat will ensure the creamiest scrambled eggs. Serve with a side of smoked salmon or crispy bacon.*

Nutritional Information (per serving):
- ✓ Calories: 250 kcal
- ✓ Fat: 22g
- ✓ Protein: 12g
- ✓ Carbohydrates: 2g

2. Ham and Spinach Egg Bake

Serves: 4 | Prep: 5 minutes | Cook : 20 minutes

Ingredients:

- 6 medium eggs
- 100g cooked ham, diced ÷ 2
- 75g fresh spinach
- 100g grated cheddar cheese
- 1 tablespoon butter

Instructions:

1.Preheat your oven to 190°C (fan 170°C) and grease a baking dish with butter.
2.In a bowl, whisk the eggs and mix in the diced ham, spinach, and half of the grated cheddar cheese.
3.Pour the mixture into the prepared baking dish and top with the remaining cheese.
4.Bake for 18-20 minutes or until the egg is set and the cheese is golden.
5.Allow to cool slightly before cutting into portions and serving.

Chef's Tip: *This egg bake can be prepared ahead and stored in the fridge for a quick breakfast or lunch.*

Nutritional Information (per serving):
- ✓ Calories: 270 kcal
- ✓ Fat: 21g
- ✓ Protein: 20g
- ✓ Carbohydrates: 2g

3. Smoked Salmon and Dill Egg Bites

**Serves: 6 egg bites (3 servings) |
Prep: 5 minutes | Cook : 15 minutes**

Ingredients:

- 6 medium eggs
- 75g smoked salmon, chopped
- 1 tablespoon fresh dill, chopped
- 50g cream cheese
- ¼ teaspoon black pepper

Instructions:

1.Preheat your oven to 180°C (fan 160°C) and grease a muffin tin with a little oil or butter.
2.In a bowl, whisk the eggs and mix in the chopped smoked salmon, dill, and cream cheese.
3.Divide the mixture evenly among the muffin cups and sprinkle with black pepper.
4.Bake for 12-15 minutes, or until the egg bites are set.
5.Let them cool slightly before removing from the tin.

Chef's Tip: *These egg bites are great for a quick breakfast or snack. Store in the fridge and reheat as needed.*

Nutritional Information (per serving):
✓ Calories: 200 kcal
✓ Fat: 16g
✓ Protein: 13g
✓ Carbohydrates: 1g

4. Cheesy Cauliflower Rice with Fried Egg

Serves: 2 | Prep: 5 minutes | Cook : 10 minutes

Ingredients:

- 300g cauliflower rice
- 50g grated cheddar cheese
- 1 tablespoon butter
- 2 medium eggs
- ¼ teaspoon salt

Instructions:

1.Heat the butter in a frying pan over medium heat. Add the cauliflower rice and cook for 5-6 minutes until tender.
2.Stir in the grated cheddar cheese and cook for an additional 1-2 minutes until melted.
3.In a separate pan, fry the eggs to your liking.
4.Serve the cheesy cauliflower rice topped with the fried eggs and season with salt.

Chef's Tip: *Cauliflower rice is a great low-carb substitute for regular rice. You can find it pre-packaged in most supermarkets, or make your own by grating fresh cauliflower.*

Nutritional Information (per serving):
✓ Calories: 250 kcal
✓ Fat: 20g
✓ Protein: 13g
✓ Carbohydrates: 3g

5. Herb and Parmesan Deviled Eggs

Serves: 4 | Prep: 5 minutes | Cook : 10 minutes

Ingredients:

- 6 medium eggs
- 2 tablespoons mayonnaise
- 1 tablespoon fresh parsley, chopped
- 25g grated Parmesan cheese
- ¼ teaspoon black pepper

Instructions:

1. Place the eggs in a saucepan and cover with cold water. Bring to a boil over medium heat, then reduce the heat and simmer for 8 minutes.
2. Drain the eggs and transfer to a bowl of cold water. Once cooled, peel the eggs and cut them in half lengthwise.
3. Remove the yolks and place them in a bowl. Mash the yolks with a fork, then add the mayonnaise, parsley, Parmesan, and black pepper. Mix until smooth.
4. Spoon or pipe the yolk mixture back into the egg whites.
5. Garnish with extra parsley if desired and serve.

Chef's Tip: *These deviled eggs make a great party snack or appetiser. Adjust the seasoning to taste, adding a pinch of smoked paprika for extra flavour.*

Nutritional Information (per serving):

- ✓ Calories: 160 kcal
- ✓ Fat: 13g
- ✓ Protein: 10g
- ✓ Carbohydrates: 1g

6. Crispy Bacon Egg and Cheese Roll-Ups

Serves: 2 | Prep: 5 minutes | Cook : 10 minutes

Ingredients:

- 4 slices streaky bacon
- 4 medium eggs
- 100g grated cheddar cheese
- 1 tablespoon butter
- ¼ teaspoon black pepper

Instructions:

1. Heat a large frying pan over medium heat and cook the bacon until crispy. Remove from the pan and set aside.
2. In the same pan, melt the butter. Crack the eggs into the pan and cook until the whites are set but the yolks are still runny, about 3-4 minutes.
3. Sprinkle the grated cheddar cheese over the eggs and let it melt.
4. Place the crispy bacon on top of the eggs and carefully roll them up using a spatula.
5. Season with black pepper and serve immediately.

Chef's Tip: *These roll-ups are perfect for a quick breakfast. You can add a sprinkle of chopped chives for added flavour.*

Nutritional Information (per serving):

- ✓ Calories: 350 kcal
- ✓ Fat: 29g
- ✓ Protein: 20g
- ✓ Carbohydrates: 1g

7. Pepperoni and Cheese Egg Cups

**Serves: 6 cups (2 servings) |
Prep: 5 minutes | Cook : 15 minutes**

Ingredients:

- 4 large eggs
- 60g pepperoni slices
- 60g cheddar cheese, grated
- 20g unsalted butter
- Salt and pepper, to taste

Instructions:

1. Preheat your oven to 180°C (fan) and grease a muffin tin with butter.
2. Line each muffin cup with pepperoni slices, creating a base.
3. Whisk the eggs and divide the mixture between the muffin cups.
4. Top each with grated cheddar cheese.
5. Bake for 12-15 minutes, or until the eggs are set.

Tips for Maintaining Ketosis: *Pepperoni adds a nice fat boost to these cups. You can substitute it with chorizo, commonly found in UK supermarkets, for a different flavour.*

Nutritional Information (per serving):
- ✓ Calories: 320 kcal
- ✓ Fat: 27g
- ✓ Protein: 20g
- ✓ Carbohydrates: 1g

8. Egg Salad-Stuffed Avocado Boats

Serves: 2 | Prep: 10 minutes | Cook : None

Ingredients:

- 2 large eggs, hard-boiled
- 1 ripe avocado
- 30g mayonnaise (sugar-free)
- 1 tsp Dijon mustard
- Salt and pepper, to taste

Instructions:

1. Peel and chop the hard-boiled eggs and add them to a bowl.
2. Mix in the mayonnaise, Dijon mustard, salt, and pepper.
3. Cut the avocado in half and remove the pit.
4. Spoon the egg salad mixture into each avocado half and serve.

Tips for Maintaining Ketosis: *Avocado is rich in healthy fats and is a keto staple. Choose a good-quality mayonnaise without added sugars, and opt for free-range eggs for higher omega-3 content.*

Nutritional Information (per serving):
- ✓ Calories: 320 kcal
- ✓ Fat: 29g
- ✓ Protein: 8g
- ✓ Carbohydrates: 4g

9. Green Onion and Sesame Keto Omelette

Serves: 2 | Prep: 5 minutes | Cook : 5 minutes

Ingredients:

- 4 large eggs
- 30g spring onions (green onions), finely chopped
- 1 tbsp sesame oil
- 1 tsp sesame seeds
- Salt and pepper, to taste

Instructions:

1. In a bowl, whisk the eggs, salt, and pepper until well combined.
2. Heat the sesame oil in a non-stick frying pan over medium heat.
3. Add the spring onions and sauté for 1-2 minutes, until softened.
4. Pour in the egg mixture and cook until the eggs are set, about 3-4 minutes.
5. Sprinkle with sesame seeds before serving.

Chef's Tip: *Sesame oil adds a distinct flavour and healthy fats. You can use sunflower oil as a substitute if needed.*

Nutritional Information (per serving):
✓ Calories: 210 kcal
✓ Fat: 18g
✓ Protein: 12g
✓ Carbohydrates: 2g

10. Spinach and Cheese Scrambled Egg Bowls

Serves: 2 | Prep: 5 minutes | Cook : 10 minutes

Ingredients:

- 4 large eggs
- 30ml double cream
- 100g fresh spinach
- 50g feta cheese, crumbled
- 1 tbsp butter

Instructions:

1. In a medium bowl, whisk the eggs with double cream until well combined. Season with salt and pepper.
2. Heat the butter in a non-stick frying pan over medium heat. Add the spinach and cook until wilted, about 2-3 minutes.
3. Pour in the egg mixture and cook, stirring gently, until the eggs are just set but still creamy.
4. Remove from the heat and fold in the crumbled feta cheese. Serve immediately.

Chef's Tip: *To add more fat, drizzle with a little extra virgin olive oil before serving. You can also swap feta for Stilton for a richer flavour.*

Nutritional Information (per serving):
✓ Calories: 235 kcal
✓ Fat: 20g
✓ Protein: 13g
✓ Carbohydrates: 2g

11. Cheesy Keto Egg and Ham Roll-Ups

Serves: 2 | Prep: 5 minutes | Cook : 10 minutes

Ingredients:

- 4 slices cooked ham
- 4 large eggs
- 50g grated mozzarella cheese
- 1 tbsp butter
- Salt and pepper, to taste

Instructions:

1 .In a frying pan, heat the butter over medium heat. Crack the eggs into the pan and scramble until just cooked through.
2.Lay out the slices of ham on a flat surface. Divide the scrambled eggs evenly among the slices and sprinkle with grated mozzarella.
3.Roll up each ham slice tightly and place seam-side down in the frying pan. Cook for 2-3 minutes, turning occasionally, until the cheese is melted and the roll-ups are heated through.
4.Season with salt and pepper before serving.

Chef's Tip: *Use British dry-cured ham for the best flavour. These roll-ups are great for breakfast or a light lunch. For added variety, use different types of cheese, such as Red Leicester or double Gloucester.*

Nutritional Information (per serving):
- ✓ Calories: 210 kcal
- ✓ Fat: 16g
- ✓ Protein: 18g
- ✓ Carbohydrates: 1g

12. Roasted Red Pepper and Egg Bake

Serves: 2 | Prep: 5 minutes | Cook : 25 minutes

Ingredients:

- 2 large roasted red peppers (jarred or freshly roasted)
- 4 large eggs
- 50g crumbled feta cheese
- 2 tablespoons heavy cream
- 1 tablespoon olive oil

Instructions:

1.Preheat your oven to 375°F (190°C).
2.Grease a small baking dish with olive oil. Slice the roasted red peppers into wide strips and layer them evenly at the bottom of the dish.
3.In a small bowl, whisk together the heavy cream and a pinch of salt and pepper. Pour the cream mixture over the roasted red peppers.
4.Create four small wells in the pepper mixture and crack an egg into each well. Sprinkle the crumbled feta cheese evenly over the top.
5.Bake in the preheated oven for 20-25 minutes, or until the egg whites are set and the yolks are cooked to your desired consistency.
6.Remove from the oven and allow it to cool for a couple of minutes before serving.

Chef's Tip: *Serve with a side of leafy greens or avocado for an extra boost of healthy fats.*

Nutritional Information (per serving):
- ✓ Calories: 215 kcal
- ✓ Fat: 18g
- ✓ Protein: 10g
- ✓ Carbohydrates: 4g

1. Keto Vanilla Chia Pudding

Serves: 2 | Prep: 5 minutes (plus chilling time)| Cook : 0 minutes

Ingredients:

- 250ml unsweetened almond milk
- 3 tablespoons chia seeds
- 1 teaspoon vanilla extract
- 1 tablespoon erythritol or preferred keto sweetener
- 50g fresh berries (optional, for topping)

Instructions:

1.In a bowl, whisk together the almond milk, chia seeds, vanilla extract, and erythritol until well combined.
2.Cover and refrigerate for at least 2 hours, or overnight, until the mixture thickens to a pudding-like consistency.
3.Stir the chia pudding before serving and divide into two bowls.
4.Top with fresh berries if desired and serve chilled.

Chef's Tip: *Chia pudding is a versatile breakfast or dessert. You can add a pinch of cinnamon or cocoa powder for added flavour.*

Nutritional Information (per serving):
- ✓ Calories: 140 kcal
- ✓ Fat: 9g
- ✓ Protein: 4g
- ✓ Carbohydrates: 3g

2. Almond Butter and Coconut Yogurt Bowl

Serves: 1 | Prep: 5 minutes | Cook : 0 minutes

Ingredients:

- 150g unsweetened coconut yogurt
- 2 tablespoons almond butter
- 1 tablespoon chia seeds
- 1 tablespoon desiccated coconut
- 1 teaspoon erythritol or preferred keto sweetener

Instructions:

1.In a bowl, mix the coconut yogurt and almond butter until smooth.
2.Stir in the chia seeds, desiccated coconut, and erythritol.
3.Serve immediately or chill for a few minutes if preferred.

Chef's Tip: *This bowl makes a satisfying breakfast or snack. Add a few sliced almonds for extra crunch.*

Nutritional Information (per serving):
- ✓ Calories: 280 kcal
- ✓ Fat: 24g
- ✓ Protein: 5g
- ✓ Carbohydrates: 4g

3. Keto Pancakes with Butter and Syrup

**Serves: 2 (4 small pancakes) |
Prep: 5 minutes | Cook : 10 minutes**

Ingredients:

- 2 large eggs
- 50g almond flour
- 1 teaspoon baking powder
- 1 tablespoon butter (plus extra for frying)
- 1 tablespoon sugar-free syrup

Instructions:

1.In a bowl, whisk together the eggs, almond flour, baking powder, and melted butter until smooth.
2.Heat a non-stick frying pan over medium heat and add a small amount of butter.
3.Spoon the batter into the pan to form small pancakes. Cook for 2-3 minutes on each side until golden brown.
4.Serve the pancakes with a drizzle of sugar-free syrup and extra butter if desired.

Chef's Tip: *These pancakes are best enjoyed fresh. You can add a pinch of cinnamon or a few fresh berries for extra flavour.*

Nutritional Information (per serving):
- ✓ Calories: 180 kcal
- ✓ Fat: 15g
- ✓ Protein: 7g
- ✓ Carbohydrates: 2g

4. Zucchini and Almond Flour Breakfast Muffins

**Serves: 3 (6 muffins) |
Prep: 5 minutes | Cook : 20 minutes**

Ingredients:

- 150g grated zucchini (courgette)
- 100g almond flour
- 3 medium eggs
- 1 teaspoon baking powder
- 50g grated cheddar cheese

Instructions:

1.Preheat your oven to 180°C (fan 160°C) and grease a muffin tin with a bit of butter or oil.
2.In a bowl, combine the grated zucchini, almond flour, eggs, baking powder, and grated cheddar cheese. Mix until well combined.
3.Spoon the mixture evenly into the muffin cups.
4.Bake for 18-20 minutes, or until the muffins are golden and a toothpick inserted into the centre comes out clean.
5.Allow the muffins to cool slightly before removing from the tin. Serve warm or store for later.

Chef's Tip: *These muffins make a great breakfast or snack. Store in the fridge for up to 3 days, or freeze for longer storage.*

Nutritional Information (per serving):
- ✓ Calories: 210 kcal
- ✓ Fat: 17g
- ✓ Protein: 9g
- ✓ Carbohydrates: 2g

5. Keto Granola Clusters with Coconut

Serves: 4 | Prep: 5 minutes | Cook : 15 minutes

Ingredients:

- 100g mixed nuts (e.g., almonds, walnuts, pecans)
- 50g desiccated coconut
- 2 tablespoons chia seeds
- 2 tablespoons coconut oil, melted
- 1 tablespoon erythritol or preferred keto sweetener

Instructions:

1. Preheat your oven to 180°C (fan 160°C) and line a baking tray with parchment paper.
2. Roughly chop the mixed nuts and combine them with the desiccated coconut, chia seeds, melted coconut oil, and erythritol in a bowl.
3. Spread the mixture evenly onto the baking tray and press down to form clusters.
4. Bake for 12-15 minutes, or until golden brown. Let cool completely before breaking into clusters.
5. Store in an airtight container and serve as a snack or with unsweetened almond milk.

Chef's Tip: *This granola is perfect for a quick snack or breakfast. You can add a few sugar-free chocolate chips for extra flavour.*

Nutritional Information (per serving):
- ✓ Calories: 250 kcal
- ✓ Fat: 23g
- ✓ Protein: 5g
- ✓ Carbohydrates: 3g

6. Creamy Coconut Milk Porridge

Serves: 2 | Prep: 5 minutes | Cook : 10 minutes

Ingredients:

- 200ml full-fat coconut milk
- 2 tablespoons almond flour
- 1 tablespoon chia seeds
- 1 teaspoon vanilla extract
- 1 tablespoon erythritol or preferred keto sweetener

Instructions:

1. In a saucepan, combine the coconut milk, almond flour, chia seeds, vanilla extract, and erythritol.
2. Cook over medium heat, stirring constantly, for about 5-7 minutes until the mixture thickens to a porridge-like consistency.
3. Divide the porridge into two bowls and serve warm.

Chef's Tip: *This porridge is a great alternative to oats. Top with a few fresh berries or a sprinkle of cinnamon for added flavour.*

Nutritional Information (per serving):
- ✓ Calories: 210 kcal
- ✓ Fat: 19g
- ✓ Protein: 3g
- ✓ Carbohydrates: 3g

7. Peanut Butter and Chocolate Keto Fat Bombs

**Serves: 4 (8 fat bombs) |
Prep: 10 minutes (plus chilling time) | Cook : 0**

Ingredients:

- 100g smooth peanut butter (sugar-free)
- 50g coconut oil, melted
- 1 tablespoon cocoa powder
- 1 tablespoon erythritol or preferred keto sweetener
- 1 teaspoon vanilla extract

Instructions:

1.In a bowl, mix together the peanut butter, melted coconut oil, cocoa powder, erythritol, and vanilla extract until smooth.
2.Spoon the mixture into silicone moulds or an ice cube tray.
3.Freeze for at least 1 hour, or until firm.
4.Pop the fat bombs out of the moulds and store in the fridge or freezer.

Chef's Tip: *Fat bombs are perfect for a quick energy boost. You can use almond butter instead of peanut butter if preferred.*

Nutritional Information (per serving):
- ✓ Calories: 180 kcal
- ✓ Fat: 16g
- ✓ Protein: 4g
- ✓ Carbohydrates: 2g

8. Keto "Oatmeal" with Chia and Flaxseeds

Serves: 2 | Prep: 5 minutes | Cook : 5 minutes

Ingredients:

- 200ml unsweetened almond milk
- 2 tablespoons chia seeds
- 2 tablespoons ground flaxseeds
- 1 teaspoon cinnamon
- 1 tablespoon erythritol or preferred keto sweetener

Instructions:

1.In a saucepan, combine the almond milk, chia seeds, ground flaxseeds, cinnamon, and erythritol.
2.Cook over medium heat, stirring frequently, for about 4-5 minutes until the mixture thickens to an oatmeal-like consistency.
3.Divide into two bowls and serve warm.

Chef's Tip: *This keto "oatmeal" is a comforting breakfast option. You can add a dollop of almond butter or a few fresh berries for extra flavour.*

Nutritional Information (per serving):
- ✓ Calories: 150 kcal
- ✓ Fat: 10g
- ✓ Protein: 5g
- ✓ Carbohydrates: 3g

9. Smoked Salmon and Cucumber Breakfast Bites

Serves: 2 | Prep: 5 minutes | Cook : 0 minutes

Ingredients:

- 100g smoked salmon
- 100g cucumber, sliced
- 50g cream cheese
- 1 teaspoon lemon juice
- 1 tablespoon fresh dill, chopped

Instructions:

1.In a small bowl, mix the cream cheese with lemon juice and half of the chopped dill.
2.Spread a little of the cream cheese mixture onto each cucumber slice.
3.Top each slice with a small piece of smoked salmon.
4.Garnish with the remaining dill and serve immediately.

Chef's Tip: *These bites are perfect for a quick breakfast or as an appetiser. You can also use slices of radish for a bit of added crunch.*

Nutritional Information (per serving):
- ✓ Calories: 180 kcal
- ✓ Fat: 14g
- ✓ Protein: 10g
- ✓ Carbohydrates: 2g

10. Cheesy Cauliflower Hash Browns

**Serves: 2 (4 hash browns) |
Prep: 10 minutes | Cook : 15 minutes**

Ingredients:

- 200g cauliflower, grated
- 50g cheddar cheese, grated
- 1 medium egg
- 1 tablespoon almond flour
- ¼ teaspoon black pepper

Instructions:

1.Preheat your oven to 200°C (fan 180°C) and line a baking tray with parchment paper.
2.In a bowl, mix the grated cauliflower, cheddar cheese, egg, almond flour, and black pepper until well combined.
3.Form the mixture into four small patties and place them on the baking tray.
4.Bake for 12-15 minutes, or until golden brown and crispy on the edges.
5.Let cool slightly before serving.

Chef's Tip: *Serve these hash browns with a dollop of sour cream or a fried egg on top for a hearty breakfast.*

Nutritional Information (per serving):
- ✓ Calories: 150 kcal
- ✓ Fat: 11g
- ✓ Protein: 9g
- ✓ Carbohydrates: 3g

11. Keto-Friendly Cinnamon "Toast" Crisps

Serves: 2 (8 crisps)
Prep: 5 minutes | Cook : 10 minutes

Ingredients:

- 4 low-carb tortillas or wraps
- 2 tablespoons butter, melted
- 1 teaspoon ground cinnamon
- 1 tablespoon erythritol or preferred keto sweetener
- ¼ teaspoon vanilla extract

Instructions:

1.Preheat your oven to 180°C (fan 160°C) and line a baking tray with parchment paper.
2.Cut the low-carb tortillas into triangles and place them on the baking tray.
3.In a small bowl, mix the melted butter, cinnamon, erythritol, and vanilla extract.
4.Brush the tortilla triangles with the cinnamon butter mixture.
5.Bake for 8-10 minutes, or until crispy and golden. Let cool before serving

Chef's Tip: *These crisps are perfect for a sweet snack or a light dessert. Serve with a side of whipped cream.*

Nutritional Information (per serving):
- ✓ Calories: 130 kcal
- ✓ Fat: 10g
- ✓ Protein: 2g
- ✓ Carbohydrates: 3g

12. Keto Strawberry Coconut Smoothie Bowl

Serves: 2 | Prep: 5 minutes | Cook : 0 minutes

Ingredients:

- 200 g strawberries (fresh or frozen)
- 200 ml coconut milk (full-fat)
- 1 tbsp chia seeds
- 20 g shredded coconut (unsweetened)
- 1 tsp erythritol or keto-friendly sweetener (optional)

Instructions:

1.Add the strawberries, coconut milk, chia seeds, and erythritol (if using) to a blender. Blend until smooth and creamy.
2.Pour the mixture into two serving bowls.
3.Top with shredded coconut. If desired, add a few additional strawberry slices on top.
4.Serve immediately and enjoy a refreshing, high-fat, low-carb breakfast option.

Chef's Tip: *Coconut milk is a great source of healthy fats and keeps the carb count low. If strawberries aren't in season, you can substitute them with raspberries.*

Nutritional Information (per serving):
- ✓ Calories: 200 kcal
- ✓ Fat: 18g
- ✓ Protein: 2g
- ✓ Carbohydrates: 6g

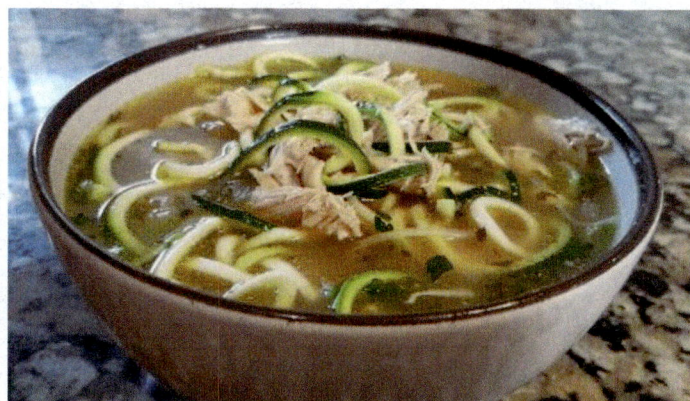

1. Creamy Broccoli Cheddar Soup

Serves: 2 | Prep: 5 minutes | Cook : 20 minutes

Ingredients:

- 300g broccoli florets
- 500ml vegetable stock
- 150g mature cheddar cheese, grated
- 100ml double cream
- 1/2 teaspoon sea salt

Instructions:

1.In a medium saucepan, bring the vegetable stock to a boil over medium heat. Add the broccoli florets and cook for about 10 minutes until they are tender.
2.Reduce the heat to low and blend the mixture with an immersion blender until smooth. If you prefer a chunkier soup, leave some pieces of broccoli whole.
3.Stir in the grated cheddar cheese and continue to stir until melted and combined.
4.Add the double cream and salt, stirring until well mixed. Let the soup simmer for another 5 minutes, making sure not to boil it to prevent the cream from curdling.
5.Serve warm, garnished with an extra sprinkle of cheddar, if desired.

Chef's Tip: *To enhance the fat content and stay in ketosis, feel free to add a tablespoon of butter for extra creaminess. For a UK twist, consider pairing this soup with a small plate of olives or sliced cucumber.*

Nutritional Information (per serving):

- ✓ Calories: 375 kcal
- ✓ Fat: 32g
- ✓ Protein: 14g
- ✓ Carbohydrates: 5g

2. Keto Chicken Zoodle Soup

Serves: 2 | Prep: 10 minutes | Cook : 15 minutes

Ingredients:

- 200g cooked chicken breast, shredded
- 400ml chicken stock
- 200g courgette (zucchini), spiralised
- 1 tablespoon olive oil
- 1/2 teaspoon dried thyme

Instructions:

1.In a medium saucepan, heat the olive oil over medium heat. Add the chicken stock and bring to a gentle simmer.
2.Add the shredded cooked chicken to the stock and cook for 5 minutes until warmed through.
3.Stir in the spiralised courgette and thyme, and simmer for another 3-4 minutes, or until the courgette is tender but not too soft.
4.Season to taste with salt and black pepper. Serve hot.

Chef's Tip: *Replace courgette with cabbage ribbons for a variation. Cabbage is a common ingredient in the UK and adds a slightly different texture while maintaining the low-carb content.*

Nutritional Information (per serving):

- ✓ Calories: 215 kcal
- ✓ Fat: 11g
- ✓ Protein: 24g
- ✓ Carbohydrates: 3g

3. 5-Minute Tomato Basil Soup

Serves: 2 | Prep: 5 minutes | Cook : 10 minutes

Ingredients:

- 400g tin chopped tomatoes
- 100ml double cream
- 200ml vegetable stock
- 10 fresh basil leaves
- 1 tablespoon olive oil

Instructions:

1.In a saucepan, heat the olive oil over medium heat. Add the chopped tomatoes and vegetable stock, and bring to a gentle simmer.
2.Add the fresh basil leaves and cook for 5 minutes to let the flavours blend.
3.Stir in the double cream, making sure not to boil the soup. Cook for an additional 2 minutes until heated through.
4.Blend the soup with an immersion blender to your desired consistency and serve hot.

Chef's Tip: *For more fat, add a drizzle of extra virgin olive oil before serving. Using good quality tinned tomatoes, such as those from Italy, will enhance the flavour of this simple yet comforting dish.*

Nutritional Information (per serving):
- ✓ Calories: 210 kcal
- ✓ Fat: 17g
- ✓ Protein: 3g
- ✓ Carbohydrates: 7g

4. Keto Creamy Mushroom Soup

Serves: 2 | Prep: 5 minutes | Cook : 20 minutes

Ingredients:

- 300g mushrooms, sliced
- 1 tablespoon butter
- 200ml double cream
- 200ml vegetable stock
- 1/2 teaspoon dried thyme

Instructions:

1.In a medium saucepan, melt the butter over medium heat. Add the sliced mushrooms and cook for 5-7 minutes, until softened and browned.
2.Pour in the vegetable stock and add the dried thyme. Bring to a gentle simmer and cook for 10 minutes.
3.Reduce the heat to low and stir in the double cream. Let it simmer for an additional 3 minutes, making sure not to boil.
4.Blend the soup to your desired consistency using an immersion blender and serve warm.

Chef's Tip: *For added fat, you can drizzle some extra virgin olive oil or add a dollop of crème fraîche before serving*

Nutritional Information (per serving):
- ✓ Calories: 285 kcal
- ✓ Fat: 26g
- ✓ Protein: 5g
- ✓ Carbohydrates: 5g

5. Spicy Sausage Kale Soup

Serves: 2 | Prep: 5 minutes | Cook : 20 minutes

Ingredients:

- 200g spicy sausage (e.g., chorizo), sliced
- 100g kale, chopped
- 400ml chicken stock
- 100ml double cream
- 1/2 teaspoon smoked paprika

Instructions:

1.In a medium saucepan, cook the sliced sausage over medium heat for 5 minutes until browned.
2.Add the chicken stock and bring to a gentle simmer. Stir in the chopped kale and cook for 10 minutes until tender.
3.Reduce the heat to low and stir in the double cream and smoked paprika. Let the soup simmer for an additional 5 minutes without boiling.
4.Serve hot, garnished with a sprinkle of smoked paprika if desired.

Chef's Tip: *If you want a thicker consistency, blend half of the soup before adding the cream. This will keep the kale texture while making the soup creamier.*

Nutritional Information (per serving):
- ✓ Calories: 350 kcal
- ✓ Fat: 30g
- ✓ Protein: 14g
- ✓ Carbohydrates: 4g

6. Creamy Cauliflower and Bacon Soup

Serves: 2 | Prep: 10 minutes | Cook : 20 minutes

Ingredients:

- 300 g cauliflower florets
- 100 g streaky bacon, chopped
- 300 ml chicken stock
- 100 ml double cream
- 1/2 teaspoon sea salt

Instructions:

1.In a saucepan over medium heat, fry the chopped bacon until crispy. Remove and set aside, leaving the bacon fat in the pan.
2.Add the cauliflower florets to the pan and sauté for 3-4 minutes in the bacon fat.
3.Pour in the chicken stock and bring to a boil. Reduce heat and simmer for 10-12 minutes, or until the cauliflower is tender.
4.Use an immersion blender to blend the soup until smooth. Stir in the double cream and sea salt.
5.Serve hot, topped with crispy bacon pieces.

Chef's Tip: *To maintain ketosis, use double cream rather than milk. For a vegetarian option, omit the bacon and use olive oil for sautéing.*

Nutritional Information (per serving):
- ✓ Calories: 320 kcal
- ✓ Fat: 28g
- ✓ Protein: 9g
- ✓ Carbohydrates: 6g

7. Roasted Red Pepper and Basil Soup

Serves: 2 | Prep: 10 minutes | Cook : 20 minutes

Ingredients:

- 2 large red peppers (about 300 g), roasted and peeled
- 300 ml vegetable stock
- 100 ml double cream
- 1 tablespoon fresh basil leaves, chopped
- 1/2 teaspoon sea salt

Instructions:

1.Roast the red peppers under a grill until the skin is charred. Peel and roughly chop.
2.In a saucepan, add the roasted peppers and vegetable stock. Bring to a boil, then reduce heat and simmer for 10 minutes.
3.Use an immersion blender to blend until smooth. Stir in the double cream, basil, and sea salt.
4.Serve hot, garnished with extra basil leaves if desired.

Chef's Tip: *Use jarred roasted red peppers for convenience. Ensure the vegetable stock is low-carb and sugar-free.*

Nutritional Information (per serving):
- ✓ Calories: 215 kcal
- ✓ Fat: 18g
- ✓ Protein: 2g
- ✓ Carbohydrates: 10g

8. Creamy Spinach and Artichoke Soup

Serves: 2 | Prep: 10 minutes | Cook : 15 minutes

Ingredients:

- 200 g fresh spinach
- 200 g artichoke hearts (jarred in water, drained)
- 300 ml vegetable stock
- 100 ml double cream
- 1/2 teaspoon sea salt

Instructions:

1.In a saucepan over medium heat, add the vegetable stock, spinach, and artichoke hearts. Bring to a boil, then reduce heat and simmer for 10 minutes.
2.Use an immersion blender to blend until smooth.
3.Stir in the double cream and sea salt. Heat through for another 2-3 minutes.
4.Serve hot.

Chef's Tip: *For a richer flavour, use chicken stock instead of vegetable stock. Ensure the artichoke hearts are packed in water, not oil.*

Nutritional Information (per serving):
- ✓ Calories: 210 kcal
- ✓ Fat: 17g
- ✓ Protein: 4g
- ✓ Carbohydrates: 8g

CHAPTER 5: Keto Salads

1. Bacon and Avocado Caesar Salad

Serves: 2 | Prep: 10 minutes

Ingredients:

- 4 rashers streaky bacon
- 1 large avocado, diced
- 100g romaine lettuce, chopped
- 50g parmesan cheese, grated
- 2 tablespoons Caesar dressing (check for low-carb options)

Instructions:

1.Cook the streaky bacon in a frying pan over medium heat until crispy. Once done, transfer to a plate lined with kitchen paper to drain excess oil.
2.In a large bowl, combine the chopped romaine lettuce, diced avocado, and half of the grated parmesan.
3.Crumble the cooked bacon into the bowl and add the Caesar dressing. Toss until all the ingredients are well coated.
4.Sprinkle the remaining parmesan cheese on top and serve immediately.

Chef's Tip: *To keep your Caesar dressing keto-friendly, ensure it contains minimal sugar. Consider making a homemade version with mayonnaise, lemon juice, and anchovies for added flavour.*

Nutritional Information (per serving):
- ✓ Calories: 405 kcal
- ✓ Fat: 36g
- ✓ Protein: 11g
- ✓ Carbohydrates: 4g

2. Shrimp and Avocado Salad

Serves: 2 | Cook : 10 minutes

Ingredients:

- 200g cooked shrimp, peeled
- 1 large avocado, diced
- 100g mixed salad leaves
- 2 tablespoons mayonnaise
- Juice of 1/2 lime

Instructions:

1.In a large bowl, combine the cooked shrimp, diced avocado, and mixed salad leaves.
2.In a small bowl, mix the mayonnaise with the lime juice until well combined.
3.Drizzle the dressing over the salad and gently toss to combine all the ingredients.
4.Season with salt and black pepper to taste, and serve immediately.

Chef's Tip: *To increase the fat content, add an extra tablespoon of mayonnaise or a drizzle of olive oil. For a different flavour, swap lime juice with lemon juice.*

Nutritional Information (per serving):
- ✓ Calories: 310 kcal
- ✓ Fat: 25g
- ✓ Protein: 15g
- ✓ Carbohydrates: 4g

3. Buffalo Chicken Salad with Ranch

Serves: 2 | Cook : 10 minutes

Ingredients:

- 200g cooked chicken breast, shredded
- 50ml buffalo sauce
- 100g mixed salad leaves
- 1 large celery stick, chopped
- 2 tablespoons ranch dressing (check for low-carb options)

Instructions:

1. In a medium bowl, combine the shredded chicken breast with the buffalo sauce until well coated.
2. In a large salad bowl, combine the mixed salad leaves and chopped celery.
3. Add the buffalo chicken on top of the salad and drizzle with ranch dressing.
4. Toss gently to combine all the ingredients and serve immediately.

Chef's Tip: *For extra fat, add sliced avocado or more ranch dressing. Make sure the buffalo sauce is sugar-free to maintain ketosis.*

Nutritional Information (per serving):

- ✓ Calories: 280 kcal
- ✓ Fat: 20g
- ✓ Protein: 22g
- ✓ Carbohydrates: 3g

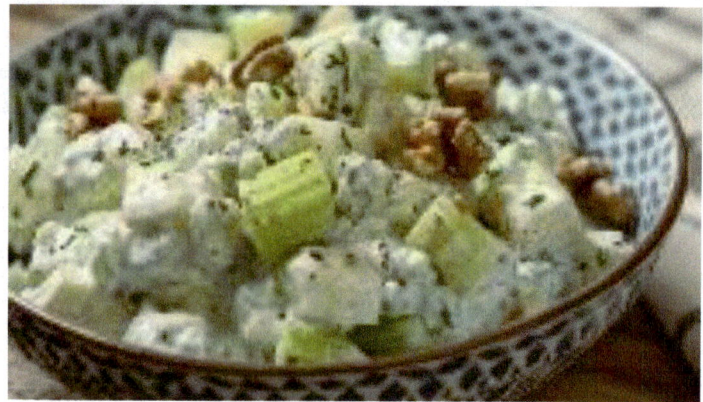

4. Keto Waldorf Salad

Serves: 2 | Cook : 10 minutes

Ingredients:

- 100g celery, chopped
- 1 large apple, diced (use a small amount to keep carbs low)
- 50g walnuts, roughly chopped
- 100g mayonnaise (full fat)
- 1 tablespoon lemon juice

Instructions:

1. In a large bowl, combine the chopped celery, diced apple, and chopped walnuts.
2. In a small bowl, mix the mayonnaise with the lemon juice until well combined.
3. Pour the dressing over the celery mixture and gently toss until evenly coated.
4. Serve immediately or chill in the fridge for 10 minutes before serving.

Chef's Tip: *To reduce the carb content, use half the amount of apple or replace it with diced cucumber. Add a sprinkle of extra chopped walnuts for more fats.*

Nutritional Information (per serving):

- ✓ Calories: 290 kcal
- ✓ Fat: 26g
- ✓ Protein: 3g
- ✓ Carbohydrates: 8g

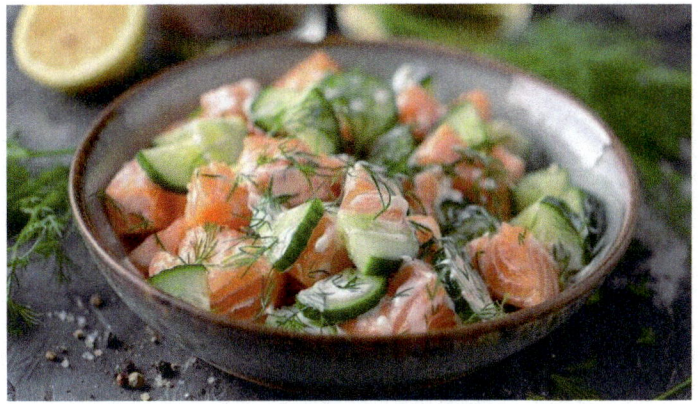

5. Zesty Italian Antipasto Salad

Serves: 2 | Cook : 10 minutes

Ingredients:

- 100g salami, sliced
- 100g mozzarella cheese, cubed
- 50g black olives
- 100g cherry tomatoes, halved
- 1 tablespoon red wine vinegar

Instructions:

1.In a large bowl, combine the sliced salami, cubed mozzarella, black olives, and cherry tomatoes.
2.Drizzle with red wine vinegar and gently toss to combine all ingredients.
3.Serve immediately or chill in the fridge for 10 minutes before serving.

Chef's Tip: *For added fats, drizzle with extra virgin olive oil. You can also add artichoke hearts or roasted red peppers for an extra Italian twist.*

Nutritional Information (per serving):
- ✓ Calories: 345 kcal
- ✓ Fat: 29g
- ✓ Protein: 16g
- ✓ Carbohydrates: 4g

6. Lemon-Dill Salmon Salad

Serves: 2 | Cook : 10 minutes

Ingredients:

- 200 g cooked salmon fillet, flaked
- 100 g cucumber, diced
- 50 g mayonnaise
- Juice of 1/2 lemon (about 1 tablespoon)
- 1 tablespoon fresh dill, chopped

Instructions:

1.In a mixing bowl, combine the flaked salmon, diced cucumber, mayonnaise, lemon juice, and chopped dill.
2.Stir well until all ingredients are evenly mixed.
3.Taste and adjust seasoning as needed with salt and pepper.
4.Serve immediately or chill in the fridge for 10 minutes before serving..

Chef's Tip: *Use freshly cooked salmon or even canned salmon (in brine) for convenience. Opt for high-quality mayonnaise made with olive oil for an added health boost.*

Nutritional Information (per serving):
- ✓ Calories: 315 kcal
- ✓ Fat: 26g
- ✓ Protein: 18g
- ✓ Carbohydrates: 2g

7. Spicy Cabbage Slaw with Jalapeño

Serves: 2 | Cook : 10 minutes

Ingredients:

- 200 g white cabbage, finely shredded
- 1 fresh jalapeño, deseeded and finely chopped
- 50 g full-fat sour cream
- 1 tablespoon apple cider vinegar
- 1/2 teaspoon sea salt

Instructions:

1.In a large mixing bowl, combine the shredded cabbage and chopped jalapeño.
2.Add the sour cream, apple cider vinegar, and sea salt.
3.Mix thoroughly until the cabbage is evenly coated.
4.Let the slaw sit for 5-10 minutes to allow the flavours to meld together.
5.Serve as a side dish or as a topping for grilled meats.

Chef's Tip: *For a spicier kick, leave some seeds in the jalapeño. You can also substitute sour cream with Greek yoghurt if preferred.*

Nutritional Information (per serving):
- ✓ Calories: 120 kcal
- ✓ Fat: 10g
- ✓ Protein: 2g
- ✓ Carbohydrates: 6g

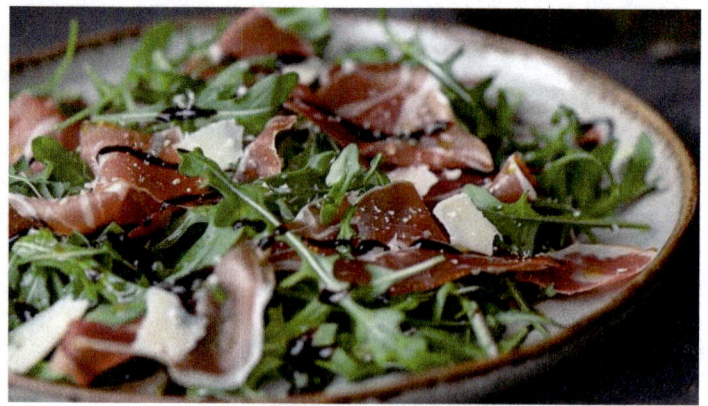

8. Prosciutto and Arugula Salad with Balsamic Drizzle

Serves: 2 | Cook : 10 minutes

Ingredients:

- 50 g prosciutto, thinly sliced
- 100 g arugula (rocket)
- 50 g Parmesan cheese, shaved
- 1 tablespoon balsamic vinegar
- 1 tablespoon extra virgin olive oil

Instructions:

1.Arrange the arugula on a serving plate.
2.Top with slices of prosciutto and shaved Parmesan cheese.
3.Drizzle with balsamic vinegar and olive oil.
4.Serve immediately.

Chef's Tip: *For a keto-friendly balsamic drizzle, use a reduced amount of balsamic vinegar or look for a sugar-free alternative.*

Nutritional Information (per serving):
- ✓ Calories: 190 kcal
- ✓ Fat: 15g
- ✓ Protein: 10g
- ✓ Carbohydrates: 2g

9. Balsamic Roasted Vegetable Salad

Serves: 2 | Prep: 10 minutes | Cook : 20 minutes

Ingredients:

- 1 medium courgette (zucchini), sliced (about 200g)
- 1 red bell pepper, sliced (about 100g)
- 2 tbsp olive oil
- 1 tbsp balsamic vinegar
- 50g mixed leafy greens

Instructions:

1. Preheat the oven to 200°C. Place the courgette and bell pepper on a baking tray, drizzle with olive oil, and season with salt and pepper.
2. Roast in the oven for 20 minutes, until the vegetables are tender and slightly caramelised.
3. In a large bowl, combine the roasted vegetables with the mixed leafy greens and drizzle with balsamic vinegar.
4. Toss everything together and serve warm or at room temperature.

Chef's Tip: *Roasting vegetables enhances their natural sweetness, making this salad a tasty low-carb option. Mixed leafy greens add freshness and balance the roasted vegetables perfectly.*

Nutritional Information (per serving):
- ✓ Calories: 180 kcal
- ✓ Fat: 15g
- ✓ Protein: 2g
- ✓ Carbohydrates: 6g

10. Keto Taco Salad with Spiced Ground Beef

Serves: 2 | Prep: 10 minutes | Cook : 10 minutes

Ingredients:

- 200g ground beef (minced beef)
- 1 tsp paprika
- ½ tsp ground cumin
- 100g mixed leafy greens
- 50g Cheddar cheese, grated

Instructions:

1. Heat a frying pan over medium heat. Add the ground beef and cook for 5-6 minutes, breaking it apart with a spoon, until browned.
2. Add the paprika and ground cumin to the beef, stirring to combine, and cook for another 2-3 minutes.
3. In a large bowl, combine the mixed leafy greens with the spiced ground beef. Top with grated Cheddar cheese.
4. Serve immediately for a hearty, keto-friendly meal.

Chef's Tip: *Using a mix of spices gives the beef a rich flavour without added carbs. Opt for grass-fed beef for a higher omega-3 content.*

Nutritional Information (per serving):
- ✓ Calories: 350 kcal
- ✓ Fat: 27g
- ✓ Protein: 24g
- ✓ Carbohydrates: 3g

11. Crispy Halloumi and Avocado Salad

Serves: 2 | Prep: 10 minutes | Cook : 5 minutes

Ingredients:

- 150g halloumi cheese, sliced
- 1 tbsp olive oil
- 1 ripe avocado, sliced
- 50g mixed leafy greens
- 1 tbsp lemon juice

Instructions:

1.Heat a frying pan over medium heat. Add the olive oil and then the halloumi slices. Cook for 2-3 minutes on each side until golden and crispy.
2.In a large bowl, combine the mixed leafy greens with the sliced avocado. Add the crispy halloumi on top.
3.Drizzle with lemon juice and serve immediately.

Chef's Tip: *Halloumi adds a salty, satisfying element to the salad, while avocado provides healthy fats to keep you fuller for longer.*

Nutritional Information (per serving):
- ✓ Calories: 320 kcal
- ✓ Fat: 28g
- ✓ Protein: 12g
- ✓ Carbohydrates: 4g

12. Warm Asparagus and Prosciutto Salad

Serves: 2 | Prep: 5 minutes | Cook : 10 minutes

Ingredients:

- 200g asparagus spears, trimmed
- 4 slices prosciutto (about 60g)
- 1 tbsp olive oil
- 1 tbsp balsamic vinegar
- 30g Parmesan cheese, shaved

Instructions:

1.Heat a frying pan over medium heat. Add the olive oil and asparagus spears. Cook for 5-6 minutes, turning occasionally, until tender.
2.Remove the asparagus from the pan and wrap each spear with a slice of prosciutto.
3.Place the wrapped asparagus on a serving plate, drizzle with balsamic vinegar, and top with shaved Parmesan cheese.
4.Serve warm for a simple, elegant keto dish.

Chef's Tip: *Prosciutto adds a savoury flavour to the tender asparagus, while Parmesan gives the dish a salty, umami kick.*

Nutritional Information (per serving):
- ✓ Calories: 210 kcal
- ✓ Fat: 16g
- ✓ Protein: 11g
- ✓ Carbohydrates: 3g

13. Warm Mushroom and Spinach Salad

Serves: 2 | Prep: 10 minutes | Cook : 10 minutes

Ingredients:

- 200g mushrooms, sliced
- 2 tbsp olive oil
- 150g spinach leaves
- 1 tbsp balsamic vinegar
- 1 clove garlic, minced

Instructions:

1.Heat 1 tablespoon of olive oil in a frying pan over medium heat. Add the minced garlic and sauté for 1 minute until fragrant.

2.Add the sliced mushrooms and cook for 5-6 minutes, until tender and golden.

3.Add the spinach leaves to the pan and cook for 1-2 minutes until wilted.

4.Drizzle with balsamic vinegar, toss to combine, and serve warm.

Chef's Tip: *This warm salad is a quick way to get in greens and healthy fats. Use a mix of mushroom varieties for added flavour complexity.*

Nutritional Information (per serving):
- ✓ Calories: 170 kcal
- ✓ Fat: 14g
- ✓ Protein: 4g
- ✓ Carbohydrates: 4g

14. Avocado & Shrimp Keto Caesar Salad

Serves: 2 | Prep: 10 minutes | Cook : 10 minutes

Ingredients:

- 200g raw shrimp, peeled and deveined
- 1 tablespoon olive oil
- 1 teaspoon garlic powder
- 1 large avocado (approx. 200g), diced
- 40g Parmesan cheese, shaved

Instructions:

1.Heat a frying pan over medium heat and add the olive oil. Once heated, add the shrimp and garlic powder. Cook for 3-4 minutes on each side or until the shrimp turn pink and are fully cooked.

2.While the shrimp are cooking, halve, pit, and dice the avocado.

3.Once the shrimp are ready, combine them in a mixing bowl with the avocado and Parmesan shavings.

4.Season with salt and pepper to taste.

5.Serve immediately in a bowl for a refreshing keto lunch or dinner.

Tip: *To maintain ketosis, always use fresh, unprocessed ingredients. In the UK, you can easily find quality olive oil and fresh shrimp from supermarkets like Waitrose or Tesco.*

Nutritional Information (per serving):
- ✓ Calories: 340 kcal
- ✓ Fat: 28g
- ✓ Protein: 20g
- ✓ Carbohydrates: 4g

15. Creamy Keto Egg & Salmon Salad

Serves: 2 | Prep: 10 minutes | Cook : 8 minutes

Ingredients:

- 4 large eggs
- 100g smoked salmon
- 2 tablespoons mayonnaise
- 1 teaspoon Dijon mustard
- 1 tablespoon chopped chives

Instructions:

1.Place the eggs in a saucepan, cover with water, and bring to a boil. Cook for 8 minutes, then transfer to a bowl of cold water.
2.Once cooled, peel the eggs and chop them into small pieces.
3.In a bowl, combine the chopped eggs, smoked salmon (sliced into small strips), mayonnaise, Dijon mustard, and chives.
4.Mix everything well, ensuring the smoked salmon is evenly distributed.
5.Serve in a bowl, and garnish with extra chives if desired.

Chef's Tip: *Use free-range eggs for best flavour and freshness. Smoked salmon is commonly found in UK supermarkets; opt for organic varieties to ensure minimal additives.*

Nutritional Information (per serving):
- ✓ Calories: 320 kcal
- ✓ Fat: 27g
- ✓ Protein: 18g
- ✓ Carbohydrates: 2g

16. Bacon, Egg & Avocado Keto Cobb Salad

Serves: 2 | Prep: 10 minutes | Cook : 10 minutes

Ingredients:

- 4 slices streaky bacon
- 2 large eggs
- 1 large avocado (approx. 200g), diced
- 50g blue cheese, crumbled
- 20g mixed salad leaves

Instructions:

1.Cook the bacon in a frying pan over medium heat until crispy. Set aside to cool, then crumble.
2.Meanwhile, place the eggs in a saucepan, cover with water, and bring to a boil. Cook for 8 minutes, then transfer to cold water. Once cooled, peel and chop.
3.Arrange the mixed salad leaves on a serving plate. Top with the diced avocado, crumbled blue cheese, chopped eggs, and crumbled bacon.
4.Serve immediately.

Chef's Tip: *Blue cheese adds a strong flavour; you can substitute with feta if preferred. Ensure the bacon is nitrate-free for a healthier option.*

Nutritional Information (per serving):
- ✓ Calories: 400 kcal
- ✓ Fat: 35g
- ✓ Protein: 18g
- ✓ Carbohydrates: 3g

CHAPTER 6: Keto Poultry Recipes

1. Keto Chicken Alfredo Bake

Serves: 4 | Prep: 10 minutes | Cook : 20 minutes

Ingredients:

- 400g chicken breast, diced
- 200ml double cream
- 100g grated mature cheddar cheese
- 2 tbsp unsalted butter (30g)
- 1 tsp dried Italian herbs (5g)

Instructions:

1.Preheat the oven to 190°C (170°C fan).
2.Heat a non-stick frying pan over medium heat and add the butter. Once melted, add the diced chicken breast and cook for about 5-7 minutes until browned.
3.Stir in the double cream and herbs, letting the mixture simmer for 3 minutes.
4.Transfer the mixture to an ovenproof dish, top with grated cheddar cheese, and bake for 15 minutes, or until golden brown.
5.Serve warm with a side of sautéed spinach.

Chef's Tip: *Tip: Double cream is a perfect keto ingredient for the UK as it's rich in fat and readily available. Substitute heavy cream, if needed, for the same effect.*

Nutritional Information (per serving):
- ✓ Calories: 440 kcal
- ✓ Fat: 36g
- ✓ Protein: 25g
- ✓ Carbohydrates: 2g

2. Bacon-Wrapped Chicken Bites

Serves: 4 | Prep: 10 minutes | Cook : 20 minutes

Ingredients:

- 400g chicken breast, cut into bite-sized pieces
- 8 slices streaky bacon (about 200g)
- 1 tsp smoked paprika (5g)
- 1 tbsp olive oil (15 ml)
- 1 tsp sea salt (5g)

Instructions:

1.Preheat the oven to 200°C (180°C fan).
2.Wrap each piece of chicken with a slice of bacon and secure with a toothpick.
3.In a small bowl, mix the olive oil, smoked paprika, and sea salt.
4.Brush each bacon-wrapped chicken bite with the olive oil mixture.
5.Arrange the chicken bites on a baking tray lined with parchment paper and bake for 20 minutes, or until the bacon is crispy and the chicken is cooked through.

Chef's Tip: *Streaky bacon is ideal for wrapping as it crisps up nicely in the oven. Serve with a simple green salad for a complete meal.*

Nutritional Information (per serving):
- ✓ Calories: 350 kcal
- ✓ Fat: 24g
- ✓ Protein: 30g
- ✓ Carbohydrates: 1g

3. Thai Coconut Chicken Curry

Serves: 4 | Prep: 5 minutes | Cook : 20 minutes

Ingredients:

- 400g chicken breast, diced
- 200ml coconut milk
- 1 tbsp red curry paste (15g)
- 1 tbsp coconut oil (15g)
- 1 tbsp fish sauce (15 ml)

Instructions:

1.Heat the coconut oil in a frying pan over medium heat.
2.Add the diced chicken and cook for 5-7 minutes, until browned.
3.Stir in the red curry paste and cook for 1 minute until fragrant.
4.Pour in the coconut milk and fish sauce, stirring to combine.
5.Simmer for 10-12 minutes, or until the chicken is cooked through and the sauce has thickened slightly. Serve with cauliflower rice.

Chef's Tip: *Coconut milk is a great source of fat for keto. Use full-fat coconut milk for the best results.*

Nutritional Information (per serving):
- ✓ Calories: 340 kcal
- ✓ Fat: 24g
- ✓ Protein: 27g
- ✓ Carbohydrates: 3g

4. Chicken Fajita Skillet

Serves: 2 | Prep: 5 minutes | Cook : 20 minutes

Ingredients:

- 400g chicken breast, sliced
- 2 bell peppers (red and green), sliced (200g)
- 1 large onion, sliced (150g)
- 2 tbsp olive oil (30 ml)
- 1 tbsp fajita seasoning (15g)

Instructions:

1.Heat olive oil in a large frying pan over medium heat.
2.Add the sliced onion and bell peppers, cooking for 3-4 minutes until softened.
3.Add the sliced chicken breast and fajita seasoning, stirring to coat the chicken and vegetables.
4.Cook for an additional 10-12 minutes, or until the chicken is cooked through.
5.Serve with sour cream or guacamole for added fat content.

Chef's Tip: *Bell peppers add colour and flavour without too many carbs. Substitute with courgettes if preferred.*

Nutritional Information (per serving):
- ✓ Calories: 250 kcal
- ✓ Fat: 16g
- ✓ Protein: 21g
- ✓ Carbohydrates: 5g

5. Crispy Sesame Chicken Tenders

Serves: 4 | Prep: 5 minutes | Cook : 20 minutes

Ingredients:

- 400g chicken breast, cut into strips
- 3 tbsp sesame seeds (30g)
- 2 tbsp olive oil (30 ml)
- 1 tsp garlic powder (5g)
- 1 tsp sea salt (5g)

Instructions:

1. Preheat the oven to 200°C (180°C fan).
2. In a large mixing bowl, combine the chicken strips, sesame seeds, olive oil, garlic powder, and sea salt.
3. Toss until the chicken is well coated.
4. Arrange the chicken tenders on a baking tray lined with parchment paper and bake for 15-20 minutes, or until golden and crispy.
5. Serve with a side of keto-friendly mayonnaise for dipping.

Chef's Tip: *Sesame seeds add a nutty flavour and crunchy texture, making these tenders a delicious keto-friendly snack or main.*

Nutritional Information (per serving):
- ✓ Calories: 310 kcal
- ✓ Fat: 20g
- ✓ Protein: 28g
- ✓ Carbohydrates: 2g

6. Creamy Garlic Mushroom Chicken

Serves: 4 | Prep: 10 minutes | Cook : 20 minutes

Ingredients:

- 4 boneless, skinless chicken breasts (600g total)
- 200g mushrooms, sliced
- 150ml double cream
- 3 cloves garlic, minced
- 2 tbsp olive oil

Instructions:

1. Heat 1 tablespoon of olive oil in a large frying pan over medium-high heat. Add the chicken breasts and cook for about 5-6 minutes per side until golden and cooked through. Remove and set aside.
2. In the same pan, add another tablespoon of olive oil and the sliced mushrooms. Sauté for about 4-5 minutes until softened.
3. Add the minced garlic and cook for an additional minute until fragrant.
4. Pour in the double cream, stir well, and simmer for 2-3 minutes until the sauce thickens slightly.
5. Return the chicken breasts to the pan, coating them in the creamy mushroom sauce. Cook for another 2-3 minutes until everything is heated through.
6. Serve immediately, garnished with a sprinkle of fresh herbs if desired.

Chef's Tip: *Use chestnut mushrooms for a deeper flavour, and serve with steamed green beans or cauliflower rice to keep it keto-friendly.*

Nutritional Information (per serving):
- ✓ Calories: 350 kcal
- ✓ Fat: 25g
- ✓ Protein: 28g
- ✓ Carbohydrates: 3g

7. Crispy Chicken Skin Chips with Dipping Sauce

Serves: 4 | Prep: 5 minutes | Cook : 20 minutes

Ingredients:

- Skin from 4 chicken breasts (about 200g)
- 1 tbsp olive oil
- 1/2 tsp sea salt
- 1/2 tsp smoked paprika
- 100g full-fat Greek yoghurt (for dipping)

Instructions:

1. Preheat the oven to 200°C (180°C fan/gas mark 6).
2. Place the chicken skins on a baking tray lined with parchment paper. Brush with olive oil and sprinkle with sea salt and smoked paprika.
3. Bake in the preheated oven for 15-20 minutes, or until crispy and golden.
4. While the skins are baking, prepare the dipping sauce by stirring the smoked paprika into the Greek yoghurt.
5. Serve the crispy chicken skin chips with the yoghurt dipping sauce.

Chef's Tip: *Save chicken skins from other recipes to make this quick keto snack, which pairs well with a tangy Greek yoghurt dip.*

Nutritional Information (per serving):
- ✓ Calories: 180 kcal
- ✓ Fat: 14g
- ✓ Protein: 11g
- ✓ Carbohydrates: 1g

8. Garlic Butter Chicken Bites with Broccoli

Serves: 4 | Prep: 10 minutes | Cook : 15 minutes

Ingredients:

- 4 boneless, skinless chicken breasts (600g total), cut into bite-sized pieces
- 2 tbsp butter
- 3 cloves garlic, minced
- 300g broccoli florets
- 1 tbsp olive oil

Instructions:

1. Heat olive oil in a large frying pan over medium-high heat. Add the chicken bites and cook for 5-6 minutes until browned and cooked through. Remove and set aside.
2. In the same pan, add the butter and minced garlic. Sauté for 1 minute until fragrant.
3. Add the broccoli florets and cook for 4-5 minutes until tender but still crisp.
4. Return the chicken to the pan and toss with the garlic butter and broccoli until well coated.
5. Serve immediately.

Chef's Tip: *Substitute broccoli with green beans or asparagus for a different twist.*

Nutritional Information (per serving):
- ✓ Calories: 300 kcal
- ✓ Fat: 20g
- ✓ Protein: 28g
- ✓ Carbohydrates: 3g

9. Smoky Paprika Chicken Wings

Serves: 4 | Prep: 5 minutes | Cook : 25 minutes

Ingredients:

- 1kg chicken wings
- 2 tbsp olive oil
- 1 tsp smoked paprika
- 1/2 tsp garlic powder
- 1/2 tsp sea salt

Instructions:

1. Preheat the oven to 200°C (180°C fan/gas mark 6).
2. In a large bowl, combine the olive oil, smoked paprika, garlic powder, and sea salt.
3. Add the chicken wings to the bowl and toss to coat evenly.
4. Place the wings on a baking tray lined with parchment paper. Bake in the preheated oven for 25-30 minutes, turning halfway through, until crispy and cooked through.
5. Serve hot.

Chef's Tip: *Serve with a side of celery sticks and a keto-friendly dip like blue cheese or ranch.*

Nutritional Information (per serving):
- ✓ Calories: 400 kcal
- ✓ Fat: 30g
- ✓ Protein: 28g
- ✓ Carbohydrates: 1g

10. Balsamic Glazed Chicken Thighs

Serves: 4 | Prep: 10 minutes | Cook : 20 minutes

Ingredients:

- 4 boneless, skin-on chicken thighs (500g total)
- 3 tbsp balsamic vinegar
- 2 tbsp olive oil
- 1 tbsp granulated erythritol
- 1 tsp dried thyme

Instructions:

1. In a small bowl, whisk together the balsamic vinegar, erythritol, and dried thyme.
2. Heat the olive oil in a large frying pan over medium-high heat. Add the chicken thighs, skin side down, and cook for 6-7 minutes until the skin is crispy.
3. Flip the chicken thighs and pour the balsamic mixture over them. Cook for another 6-7 minutes until the chicken is cooked through and the glaze has thickened.
4. Serve hot, garnished with a sprinkle of fresh thyme if desired.

Chef's Tip: *Serve with roasted courgettes or a side of green beans to keep it keto-friendly..*

Nutritional Information (per serving):
- ✓ Calories: 320 kcal
- ✓ Fat: 24g
- ✓ Protein: 22g
- ✓ Carbohydrates: 3g

11. Quick Parmesan-Crusted Chicken Breasts

Serves: 4 | Prep: 5 minutes | Cook : 15 minutes

Ingredients:

- 4 boneless, skinless chicken breasts (600g total)
- 100g grated Parmesan cheese
- 1 tsp dried Italian herbs
- 2 tbsp olive oil
- 1/2 tsp sea salt

Instructions:

1. Preheat the oven to 200°C (180°C fan/gas mark 6).
2. In a bowl, mix the grated Parmesan, dried Italian herbs, and sea salt.
3. Brush the chicken breasts with olive oil, then coat them in the Parmesan mixture.
4. Place the chicken breasts on a baking tray lined with parchment paper. Bake in the preheated oven for 15 minutes or until golden and cooked through.
5. Serve hot.

Chef's Tip: *Serve with a side of roasted vegetables or a simple green salad to complete your meal.*

Nutritional Information (per serving):

- ✓ Calories: 310 kcal
- ✓ Fat: 20g
- ✓ Protein: 32g
- ✓ Carbohydrates: 1g

12. Savory Stuffed Chicken Thighs with Mushrooms & Bacon

Serves: 4 | Prep: 10 minutes | Cook : 20 minutes

Ingredients:

- 4 large skin-on, boneless chicken thighs (approximately 600 g total)
- 100 g chestnut mushrooms, finely chopped
- 2 rashers streaky bacon, diced
- 50 g full-fat cream cheese
- 2 tbsp olive oil
- Sea salt and freshly ground black pepper, to taste

Instructions:

1. Heat 1 tablespoon of olive oil in a frying pan over medium heat. Add the diced bacon and cook for 2-3 minutes until golden and crispy. Stir in the mushrooms and cook for an additional 3-4 minutes until softened. Remove from heat and mix in the cream cheese until well combined. Season with a pinch of salt and black pepper. Set aside to cool slightly.
2. Pat the chicken thighs dry with kitchen paper. Place them skin-side down on a chopping board. Spoon an equal amount of the mushroom and bacon filling onto each thigh. Fold the edges over to seal the stuffing inside, securing with toothpicks if necessary.
3. Heat the remaining olive oil in a large oven-safe frying pan over medium-high heat. Place the chicken thighs skin-side down and cook for 4-5 minutes until the skin is golden and crispy. Turn the thighs over, reduce the heat to medium, and cook for another 3-4 minutes. Transfer the pan to a preheated oven (180°C fan/200°C conventional) and bake for 10 minutes until the chicken is cooked through and the juices run clear.
4. Remove the chicken thighs from the oven and let them rest for 5 minutes. Serve with steamed broccoli or a side salad drizzled with olive oil for a complete keto meal.

Nutritional Information (per serving):

- ✓ Calories: 250 kcal
- ✓ Fat: 22g
- ✓ Protein: 12g
- ✓ Carbohydrates: 2g

1. Garlic Butter Steak Bites

Serves: 4 | Prep: 5 minutes | Cook : 10 minutes

Ingredients:

- 500g sirloin steak, cut into bite-sized pieces
- 3 tablespoons unsalted butter
- 3 cloves garlic, minced
- 1 tablespoon olive oil
- Salt and pepper, to taste

Instructions:

1. Heat olive oil in a large frying pan over medium-high heat.
2. Season the steak bites with salt and pepper. Add to the pan and cook for 2-3 minutes until browned.
3. Reduce the heat to medium. Add the butter and minced garlic, cooking for an additional 2-3 minutes while stirring the steak bites in the garlic butter.
4. Serve immediately.

Chef's Tip: *Serve with a side of steamed broccoli or cauliflower mash for a complete meal. Use grass-fed butter for added health benefits.*

Nutritional Information (per serving):
- ✓ Calories: 320 kcal
- ✓ Fat: 25g
- ✓ Protein: 23g
- ✓ Carbohydrates: 1g

2. Pork Chops with Creamy Mustard Sauce

Serves: 4 | Prep: 5 minutes | Cook : 20 minutes

Ingredients:

- 4 bone-in pork chops (600g total)
- 2 tablespoons Dijon mustard
- 100ml double cream
- 1 tablespoon olive oil
- Salt and pepper, to taste

Instructions:

1. Heat olive oil in a large frying pan over medium heat. Season the pork chops with salt and pepper.
2. Cook the pork chops for 5-6 minutes per side, or until cooked through. Remove from the pan and set aside.
3. Lower the heat to medium-low. Add the double cream and Dijon mustard to the pan, stirring to combine.
4. Return the pork chops to the pan and cook for an additional 2-3 minutes, spooning the sauce over the chops.

Chef's Tip: *Serve with a side of sautéed spinach or cabbage to keep it low-carb. Double cream adds richness and helps maintain ketosis.*

Nutritional Information (per serving):
- ✓ Calories: 380 kcal
- ✓ Fat: 30g
- ✓ Protein: 25g
- ✓ Carbohydrates: 1g

3. Keto Beef Stroganoff

Serves: 4 | Prep: 5 minutes | Cook : 20 minutes

Ingredients:

- 400g beef sirloin, sliced into strips
- 100g mushrooms, sliced
- 100ml double cream
- 1 tablespoon butter
- 1 teaspoon smoked paprika

Instructions:

1. Heat butter in a large frying pan over medium heat. Add the sliced beef and cook for 3-4 minutes until browned.
2. Add the mushrooms and cook for an additional 5 minutes until softened.
3. Stir in the double cream and smoked paprika, cooking for another 2-3 minutes until the sauce thickens.
4. Serve immediately.

Chef's Tip: *Serve over cauliflower rice or shirataki noodles to keep it low-carb. Double cream helps to add fat and maintain a creamy consistency.*

Nutritional Information (per serving):

- ✓ Calories: 340 kcal
- ✓ Fat: 27g
- ✓ Protein: 22g
- ✓ Carbohydrates: 3g

4. Parmesan-Crusted Pork Medallions

Serves: 4 | Prep: 10 minutes | Cook : 20 minutes

Ingredients:

- 500g pork tenderloin, cut into medallions
- 50g grated Parmesan cheese
- 1 teaspoon dried thyme
- 2 tablespoons olive oil
- Salt and pepper, to taste

Instructions:

1. Preheat oven to 200°C (180°C fan/gas mark 6).
2. Season the pork medallions with salt, pepper, and dried thyme.
3. Press each medallion into the grated Parmesan cheese to coat both sides.
4. Heat olive oil in a large ovenproof frying pan over medium heat. Sear the pork medallions for 2-3 minutes per side, until golden.
5. Transfer the pan to the preheated oven and bake for 10-12 minutes until the pork is fully cooked.

Chef's Tip: *Use full-fat Parmesan and a good quality pork tenderloin to maintain your fat intake. If Parmesan isn't available, mature cheddar can work well.*

Nutritional Information (per serving):

- ✓ Calories: 230 kcal
- ✓ Fat: 15g
- ✓ Protein: 23g
- ✓ Carbohydrates: 1g

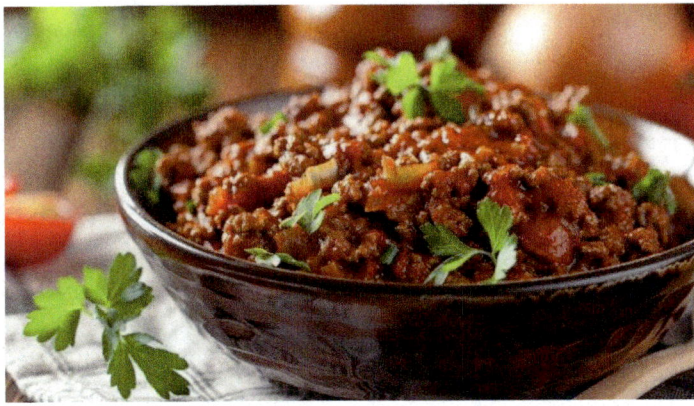

5. Keto Sloppy Joes

Serves: 4 | Prep: 5 minutes | Cook : 20 minutes

Ingredients:

- 400g minced beef
- 1 medium onion, finely chopped (120g)
- 200g tomato passata
- 1 tablespoon Worcestershire sauce
- 1 tablespoon butter

Instructions:

1.Heat a large frying pan over medium heat and melt the butter.
2.Add the chopped onion and cook for 3-4 minutes until softened.
3.Add the minced beef and cook until browned, breaking it up with a spoon.
4.Stir in the tomato passata and Worcestershire sauce, and simmer for 10-12 minutes until thickened.

Chef's Tip: *Serve on lettuce leaves for a low-carb alternative to buns. Worcestershire sauce in the UK is typically sugar-free, but double-check labels.*

Nutritional Information (per serving):
- ✓ Calories: 320 kcal
- ✓ Fat: 24g
- ✓ Protein: 21g
- ✓ Carbohydrates: 5g

6. Crispy Pork Belly with Garlic Butter

Serves: 4 | Prep: 10 minutes | Cook : 30 minutes

Ingredients:

- 600g pork belly, skin scored
- 2 tablespoons olive oil
- 2 cloves garlic, minced
- 2 tablespoons unsalted butter
- Salt and pepper, to taste

Instructions:

1.Preheat oven to 220°C (200°C fan/gas mark 7).
2.Rub the pork belly with olive oil, salt, and pepper. Place in a roasting tray, skin side up.
3.Roast for 25-30 minutes until the skin is crispy.
4.In a small saucepan, melt the butter over low heat and add the minced garlic. Cook for 1-2 minutes until fragrant.
5.Drizzle the garlic butter over the crispy pork belly before serving.

Chef's Tip: *Make sure the pork skin is well-scored to achieve maximum crispiness. Serve with a side of steamed greens for added fibre.*

Nutritional Information (per serving):
- ✓ Calories: 450 kcal
- ✓ Fat: 40g
- ✓ Protein: 20g
- ✓ Carbohydrates: 1g

7. Keto Salisbury Steak with Gravy

Serves: 4 | Prep: 10 minutes | Cook : 20 minutes

Ingredients:

- 500g minced beef
- 1 teaspoon dried onion powder
- 1 teaspoon dried garlic powder
- 100ml double cream
- 1 tablespoon butter

Instructions:

1.In a bowl, mix the minced beef, onion powder, and garlic powder. Form into 4 patties.
2.Heat a frying pan over medium heat and melt the butter. Cook the patties for 4-5 minutes per side until browned.
3.Remove the patties from the pan and set aside. Add the double cream to the pan, stirring to create a gravy.
4.Return the patties to the pan and cook for an additional 3-4 minutes until the gravy thickens.

Chef's Tip: *Double cream is a great way to add fat content to your keto meals. Serve with cauliflower mash for a classic comfort dish.*

Nutritional Information (per serving):
- ✓ Calories: 370 kcal
- ✓ Fat: 31g
- ✓ Protein: 21g
- ✓ Carbohydrates: 2g

8. Bacon Cheeseburger Casserole

Serves: 4 | Prep: 5 minutes | Cook : 25 minutes

Ingredients:

- 400g minced beef
- 100g bacon, chopped
- 100g grated cheddar cheese
- 2 tablespoons tomato purée
- 1 tablespoon Dijon mustard

Instructions:

1.Preheat oven to 200°C (180°C fan/gas mark 6).
2.In a frying pan, cook the chopped bacon over medium heat until crispy. Remove and set aside.
3.Add the minced beef to the same pan and cook until browned, about 5-6 minutes.
4.Stir in the tomato purée and Dijon mustard, then transfer to a baking dish.
5.Top with grated cheddar and bacon, and bake for 10-12 minutes until the cheese is melted and bubbly.

Chef's Tip: *Use smoked bacon for added flavour. This dish pairs well with a simple green salad.*

Nutritional Information (per serving):
- ✓ Calories: 400 kcal
- ✓ Fat: 32g
- ✓ Protein: 25g
- ✓ Carbohydrates: 3g

9. Keto Korean Beef Bowls

Serves: 4 | Prep: 5 minutes | Cook : 15 minutes

Ingredients:

- 400g minced beef
- 2 tablespoons tamari (gluten-free soy sauce alternative)
- 1 tablespoon sesame oil
- 1 teaspoon grated ginger
- 2 spring onions, sliced (20g)

Instructions:

1. Heat sesame oil in a frying pan over medium heat. Add the minced beef and cook for 5-6 minutes until browned.
2. Stir in the tamari and grated ginger, cooking for an additional 3-4 minutes.
3. Top with sliced spring onions before serving.

Chef's Tip: *Serve over shredded cabbage or cauliflower rice to keep it low-carb. Adjust ginger to taste for extra spice.*

Nutritional Information (per serving):
- ✓ Calories: 300 kcal
- ✓ Fat: 22g
- ✓ Protein: 21g
- ✓ Carbohydrates: 2g

10. Herb-Crusted Pork Chops with Garlic Butter

Serves: 2 | Prep: 10 minutes | Cook : 20 minutes

Ingredients:

- 2 pork chops (around 200g each)
- 20g fresh rosemary and thyme, finely chopped
- 50g unsalted butter
- 2 garlic cloves, minced
- Salt and pepper, to taste

Instructions:

1. Preheat the oven to 190°C (170°C fan). Season both sides of the pork chops with salt, pepper, and the chopped rosemary and thyme.
2. In a heavy-bottomed frying pan, heat half of the butter over medium heat until melted. Add the pork chops and cook for 3-4 minutes per side, until browned.
3. Transfer the pork chops to a baking tray and place in the preheated oven for about 10 minutes, or until the internal temperature reaches 63°C.
4. While the pork chops are in the oven, melt the remaining butter in the frying pan, then add the minced garlic. Cook for 1-2 minutes until fragrant but not browned.
5. Drizzle the garlic butter over the pork chops before serving.

Chef's Tip: *Pair with a side of steamed broccoli and a dollop of butter for a filling, low-carb meal.*

Nutritional Information (per serving):
- ✓ Calories: 425 kcal
- ✓ Fat: 35g
- ✓ Protein: 25g
- ✓ Carbohydrates: 1g

11. Keto Beef Fajita Skillet

Serves: 2 | Prep: 5 minutes | Cook : 20 minutes

Ingredients:

- 300g beef steak, sliced thinly
- 1 red bell pepper, sliced
- 1 green bell pepper, sliced
- 2 tbsp olive oil
- 1 tsp smoked paprika

Instructions:

1.Heat a large frying pan over medium-high heat and add 1 tablespoon of olive oil. Add the sliced beef and cook for 5-6 minutes until browned. Remove from the pan and set aside.
2.Add the remaining olive oil to the pan, then add the sliced bell peppers. Cook for 5-7 minutes until softened.
3.Return the beef to the pan and sprinkle with smoked paprika. Stir well to combine, and cook for an additional 2-3 minutes until everything is heated through.
4.Serve immediately, garnished with extra paprika if desired.

Chef's Tip: *Serve with a dollop of sour cream for added fat content, and use mixed bell peppers to add colour and variety.*

Nutritional Information (per serving):
- ✓ Calories: 380 kcal
- ✓ Fat: 28g
- ✓ Protein: 27g
- ✓ Carbohydrates: 4g

12. Keto Pork Cutlets with Creamy Herb Sauce

Serves: 2 | Prep: 10 minutes | Cook : 20 minutes

Ingredients:

- 2 pork cutlets (around 200g each)
- 100ml double cream
- 1 tbsp Dijon mustard
- 1 tbsp olive oil
- 1 tsp dried parsley

Instructions:

1.Season the pork cutlets with salt and pepper. Heat the olive oil in a large frying pan over medium heat.
2.Add the pork cutlets to the pan and cook for 5-6 minutes per side, or until cooked through. Remove from the pan and set aside.
3.In the same pan, add the double cream, Dijon mustard, and dried parsley. Stir well and let it simmer for 2-3 minutes until slightly thickened.
4.Return the pork cutlets to the pan, spooning the creamy herb sauce over them. Serve hot.

Chef's Tip: *Serve with steamed asparagus or green beans to keep carbs low while adding fibre.*

Nutritional Information (per serving):
- ✓ Calories: 490 kcal
- ✓ Fat: 38g
- ✓ Protein: 27g
- ✓ Carbohydrates: 2g

13. Beef and Cabbage Stir-Fry

Serves: 2 | Prep: 5 minutes | Cook : 15 minutes

Ingredients:

- 300g minced beef
- 200g shredded cabbage
- 2 tbsp soy sauce (or tamari for gluten-free)
- 1 tbsp sesame oil
- 1 tsp ground ginger

Instructions:

1.Heat a large frying pan or wok over medium heat. Add the sesame oil and minced beef, cooking for 8-10 minutes until browned.
2.Add the shredded cabbage and cook for another 3-4 minutes until softened.
3.Stir in the soy sauce and ground ginger, mixing well. Cook for an additional 2 minutes.
4.Serve immediately.

Chef's Tip: *Cabbage is a low-carb vegetable that adds bulk to meals without many carbs. Use tamari for a gluten-free option.*

Nutritional Information (per serving):

- ✓ Calories: 400 kcal
- ✓ Fat: 30g
- ✓ Protein: 25g
- ✓ Carbohydrates: 5g

14. Keto Ground Beef and Cheese Skillet

Serves: 2 | Prep: 5 minutes | Cook : 20 minutes

Ingredients:

- 300g minced beef
- 100g grated cheddar cheese
- 1 small onion, finely chopped
- 1 tbsp olive oil
- Salt and pepper, to taste

Instructions:

1.Heat the olive oil in a large frying pan over medium heat. Add the chopped onion and cook for 3-4 minutes until softened.
2.Add the minced beef to the pan and cook for 8-10 minutes, breaking it apart until browned.
3.Season with salt and pepper, then sprinkle the grated cheddar cheese over the beef. Cover the pan and let the cheese melt for 2-3 minutes.
4.Serve hot, garnished with fresh herbs if desired.

Chef's Tip: *Using high-quality cheddar adds both flavour and fat, keeping this dish satisfying and keto-friendly.*

Nutritional Information (per serving):

- ✓ Calories: 520 kcal
- ✓ Fat: 40g
- ✓ Protein: 32g
- ✓ Carbohydrates: 4g

15. Pork Tenderloin with Lemon Butter

Serves: 2 | Prep: 5 minutes | Cook : 25 minutes

Ingredients:

- 300g pork tenderloin
- Juice of 1 lemon
- 50g unsalted butter
- 1 tbsp olive oil
- Salt and pepper, to taste

Instructions:

1. Preheat the oven to 190°C (170°C fan). Season the pork tenderloin with salt and pepper.
2. Heat the olive oil in an oven-safe frying pan over medium heat. Sear the pork tenderloin for 3-4 minutes on each side until browned.
3. Transfer the pan to the oven and bake for 15-20 minutes, or until the internal temperature reaches 63°C.
4. In a small saucepan, melt the butter over low heat. Stir in the lemon juice and cook for 1-2 minutes.
5. Slice the pork tenderloin and drizzle with lemon butter before serving.

Chef's Tip: *Serve with a side of roasted asparagus for a complete low-carb meal.*

Nutritional Information (per serving):
- ✓ Calories: 460 kcal
- ✓ Fat: 35g
- ✓ Protein: 30g
- ✓ Carbohydrates: 2g

16. Keto Pork Stir-Fry with Zucchini

Serves: 2 | Prep: 5 minutes | Cook : 15 minutes

Ingredients:

- 300g pork loin, thinly sliced
- 1 medium zucchini, sliced into half-moons
- 2 tbsp soy sauce (or tamari for gluten-free)
- 1 tbsp sesame oil
- 1 garlic clove, minced

Instructions:

1. Heat the sesame oil in a large frying pan or wok over medium heat. Add the minced garlic and cook for 1 minute until fragrant.
2. Add the sliced pork loin and cook for 5-6 minutes until browned.
3. Add the zucchini and cook for an additional 3-4 minutes until tender.
4. Stir in the soy sauce and cook for 1-2 more minutes until everything is well coated.
5. Serve immediately.

Chef's Tip: *Zucchini is a great low-carb vegetable that adds bulk without many carbs. Adjust seasoning to taste for a flavourful stir-fry.*

Nutritional Information (per serving):
- ✓ Calories: 420 kcal
- ✓ Fat: 28g
- ✓ Protein: 32g
- ✓ Carbohydrates: 4g

1. Garlic Parmesan Baked Scallops

Serves: 2 | Prep: 10 minutes | Cook : 15 minutes

Ingredients:

- 200g scallops
- 2 tbsp unsalted butter (30g)
- 2 cloves garlic, finely minced
- 30g grated Parmesan cheese
- 1 tbsp chopped fresh parsley (5g)

Instructions:

1. Preheat your oven to 200°C (fan-assisted).
2. In a small saucepan, melt the butter over medium heat and add the minced garlic. Cook for 1-2 minutes until fragrant.
3. Arrange the scallops in a baking dish and pour the garlic butter over them.
4. Sprinkle the grated Parmesan cheese evenly over the scallops.
5. Bake for 12-15 minutes or until the scallops are opaque and the cheese is golden.
6. Garnish with chopped parsley before serving.

Chef's Tip: *Scallops are naturally low in carbs and high in protein. The Parmesan adds a good dose of fats to balance the dish.*

Nutritional Information (per serving):

- ✓ Calories: 260 kcal
- ✓ Fat: 18g
- ✓ Protein: 21g
- ✓ Carbohydrates: 2g

2. Creamy Coconut Shrimp Curry

Serves: 2 | Prep: 5 minutes | Cook : 15 minutes

Ingredients:

- 300g raw king prawns, peeled and deveined
- 1 tbsp coconut oil (15 ml)
- 200 ml coconut milk (full fat)
- 1 tsp curry powder (5g)
- Juice of ½ lime (15 ml)

Instructions:

1. Heat the coconut oil in a large frying pan over medium heat.
2. Add the curry powder and cook for 1 minute until fragrant.
3. Stir in the coconut milk and bring to a simmer.
4. Add the prawns and cook for 5-6 minutes until pink and cooked through.
5. Stir in the lime juice and serve with cauliflower rice for a keto-friendly meal.

Chef's Tip: *Full-fat coconut milk provides a rich source of fats, perfect for staying in ketosis. Adjust the curry powder to taste.*

Nutritional Information (per serving):

- ✓ Calories: 320 kcal
- ✓ Fat: 26g
- ✓ Protein: 20g
- ✓ Carbohydrates: 3g

3. Keto Lobster Tails with Garlic Butter

Serves: 2 | Prep: 10 minutes | Cook : 15 minutes

Ingredients:

- 2 lobster tails (approx. 150g each)
- 3 tbsp unsalted butter (45g)
- 2 cloves garlic, finely minced
- Juice of ½ lemon (15 ml)
- 1 tbsp chopped fresh parsley (5g)

Instructions:

1. Preheat your oven to 200°C (fan-assisted).
2. In a small saucepan, melt the butter over medium heat and add the minced garlic. Cook for 1-2 minutes until fragrant.
3. Brush the lobster tails with the garlic butter mixture.
4. Place the lobster tails on a baking tray and bake for 12-15 minutes, or until the meat is opaque and cooked through.
5. Drizzle with lemon juice and garnish with chopped parsley before serving.

Chef's Tip: *Lobster is a great source of protein. Adding butter helps increase the fat content, making it perfect for keto.*

Nutritional Information (per serving):
- ✓ Calories: 280 kcal
- ✓ Fat: 22g
- ✓ Protein: 19g
- ✓ Carbohydrates: 1g

4. Keto Spicy Sriracha Salmon Steaks

Serves: 2 | Prep: 5 minutes | Cook : 15 minutes

Ingredients:

- 2 salmon steaks (approx. 150g each)
- 2 tbsp sriracha sauce
- 1 tbsp coconut oil, melted
- Juice of 1 lime (approximately 50ml)
- 1 tsp smoked paprika

Instructions:

1. Preheat the oven to 200°C (180°C fan/gas mark 6).
2. In a small bowl, mix together the sriracha sauce, melted coconut oil, lime juice, and smoked paprika.
3. Place the salmon steaks on a lined baking tray and brush with the sriracha mixture.
4. Bake in the preheated oven for 12-15 minutes, or until the salmon is cooked through

Chef's Tip: *Sriracha adds a spicy kick, but can be adjusted to suit your taste. Coconut oil adds a high-fat component that is essential for maintaining ketosis. Salmon is a good source of omega-3 fatty acids, making it a great choice for a balanced keto meal.*

Nutritional Information (per serving):
- ✓ Calories: 320 kcal
- ✓ Fat: 24g
- ✓ Protein: 22g
- ✓ Carbohydrates: 2g

5. Keto Herb Butter Baked Mussels

Serves: 4 | Prep: 10 minutes | Cook : 15 minutes

Ingredients:

- 1kg fresh mussels, cleaned
- 100g unsalted butter, softened
- 2 cloves garlic, minced
- 1 tbsp chopped fresh parsley
- Zest of 1 lemon

Instructions:

1.Preheat the oven to 200°C (180°C fan/gas mark 6).
2.In a small bowl, mix the softened butter, minced garlic, chopped parsley, and lemon zest.
3.Arrange the cleaned mussels in a baking dish and dot with the herb butter mixture.
4.Bake in the preheated oven for 12-15 minutes, or until the mussels have opened and are cooked through. Discard any that do not open.
5.Serve hot, spooning the melted herb butter over the mussels.

Chef's Tip: *Mussels are high in protein and low in carbs, making them an ideal keto seafood option. Fresh mussels can be easily sourced from local fishmongers in the UK.*

Nutritional Information (per serving):
- ✓ Calories: 220 kcal
- ✓ Fat: 18g
- ✓ Protein: 16g
- ✓ Carbohydrates: 2g

6. Pan-Seared Cod with Lemon-Caper Sauce

Serves: 2 | Prep: 5 minutes | Cook : 10 minutes

Ingredients:

- 2 cod fillets (approx. 150g each)
- 2 tbsp olive oil
- Juice of 1 lemon (approximately 50ml)
- 1 tbsp capers, drained
- 1 tbsp unsalted butter

Instructions:

1.Heat the olive oil in a frying pan over medium-high heat. Season the cod fillets with salt and add them to the pan.
2.Cook for 3-4 minutes per side, until the cod is golden brown and flakes easily with a fork.
3.Reduce the heat to low and add the butter, lemon juice, and capers to the pan. Stir to create a sauce.
4.Spoon the lemon-caper sauce over the cod before serving.

Chef's Tip: *Capers add a salty, tangy element that complements the cod. This dish pairs well with steamed greens for a complete keto meal.*

Nutritional Information (per serving):
- ✓ Calories: 250 kcal
- ✓ Fat: 18g
- ✓ Protein: 22g
- ✓ Carbohydrates: 1g

7. Keto Garlic Butter Squid with Roasted Bell Peppers

Serves: 2 | Prep: 10 minutes | Cook : 15 minutes

Ingredients:

- 250g squid, cleaned and sliced into rings
- 1 red bell pepper, sliced (100g)
- 50g unsalted butter
- 2 cloves garlic, finely chopped
- 1 tbsp olive oil (15ml)

Instructions:

1.Preheat your oven to 200°C (fan 180°C). Toss the sliced bell pepper with the olive oil and season lightly with salt. Place on a baking tray and roast for 10-12 minutes or until tender.
2.While the peppers are roasting, melt the butter in a large frying pan over medium heat. Add the chopped garlic and cook for 1-2 minutes until fragrant.
3.Add the squid rings to the frying pan and cook for about 3-4 minutes until they turn opaque and tender. Stir frequently to avoid overcooking the squid.
4.Serve the squid hot, with the roasted bell pepper on the side. Drizzle any extra garlic butter from the pan over the top.

Chef's Tip: *Use fresh squid for best results. Feel free to substitute the bell pepper with another keto-friendly vegetable, such as courgette or broccoli.*

Nutritional Information (per serving):
- ✓ Calories: 305 kcal
- ✓ Fat: 26g
- ✓ Protein: 14g
- ✓ Carbohydrates: 3g

8. Quick Keto Salmon Patties with Creamy Spinach

Serves: 2 | Prep: 10 minutes | Cook : 15 minutes

Ingredients:

- 200g canned salmon, drained
- 1 egg
- 1 tbsp almond flour (8g)
- 100g fresh spinach
- 2 tbsp double cream (30ml)

Instructions:

1.In a mixing bowl, combine the drained salmon, egg, and almond flour. Form the mixture into 4 small patties.
2.Heat a non-stick frying pan over medium heat and cook the patties for 3-4 minutes per side until golden brown.
3.In a separate pan, add the fresh spinach and cook over medium heat until wilted. Stir in the double cream and season with salt and pepper to taste.
4.Serve the salmon patties alongside the creamy spinach.

Chef's Tip: *If almond flour is not available, use ground flaxseed as a substitute. You can also add a squeeze of lemon to the salmon patties for a bit of extra zest.*

Nutritional Information (per serving):
- ✓ Calories: 320 kcal
- ✓ Fat: 22g
- ✓ Protein: 26g
- ✓ Carbohydrates: 2g

9. Keto Salmon Skewers with Roasted Zucchini

Serves: 2 | Prep: 10 minutes | Cook : 20 minutes

Ingredients:

- 300g salmon fillet, cut into cubes
- 1 medium zucchini, sliced (150g)
- 1 tbsp olive oil (15ml)
- 1 tsp paprika
- Juice of 1/2 lemon

Instructions:

1.Preheat your oven to 200°C (fan 180°C). Thread the salmon cubes onto skewers and brush with olive oil.
2.Sprinkle the salmon skewers with paprika and season with salt and pepper.
3.Place the sliced zucchini on a baking tray, drizzle with olive oil, and season lightly.
4.Roast the zucchini and grill the salmon skewers in the oven for 15-18 minutes, turning the skewers halfway through.
5.Serve the salmon skewers with the roasted zucchini, drizzling with lemon juice before serving.

Chef's Tip: *Soak wooden skewers in water for 20 minutes before using to prevent burning. You can also use cherry tomatoes as an additional skewer ingredient.*

Nutritional Information (per serving):
- ✓ Calories: 310 kcal
- ✓ Fat: 20g
- ✓ Protein: 27g
- ✓ Carbohydrates: 4g

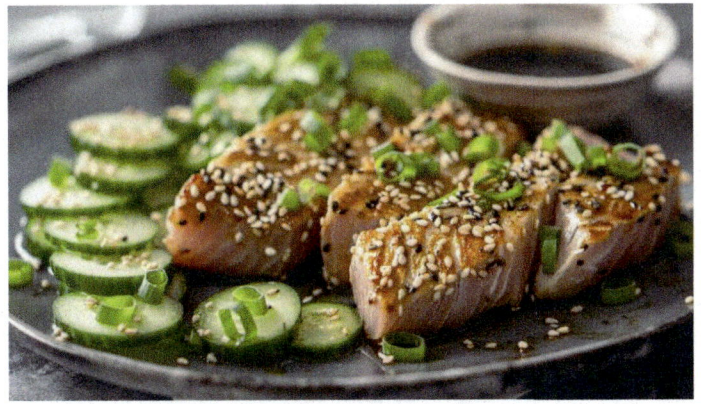

10. Keto Sesame-Crusted Tuna with Cucumber Salad

Serves: 2 | Prep: 10 minutes | Cook : 10 minutes

Ingredients:

- 2 tuna steaks (approx. 150g each)
- 2 tbsp sesame seeds (16g)
- 1 tbsp coconut oil (15ml)
- 1/2 cucumber, thinly sliced (100g)
- 1 tbsp rice vinegar (15ml)

Instructions:

1.Press the sesame seeds onto both sides of the tuna steaks.
2.Heat the coconut oil in a frying pan over medium-high heat. Add the tuna steaks and sear for 2-3 minutes per side, or until cooked to your preferred level of doneness.
3.In a small bowl, combine the cucumber slices and rice vinegar. Mix well and season with salt.
4.Serve the sesame-crusted tuna with the cucumber salad on the side.

Chef's Tip: *For a bit of spice, add a pinch of chilli flakes to the sesame seeds before coating the tuna. Rice vinegar can be substituted with white wine vinegar if unavailable.*

Nutritional Information (per serving):
- ✓ Calories: 320 kcal
- ✓ Fat: 22g
- ✓ Protein: 28g
- ✓ Carbohydrates: 3g

11. Garlic Butter Shrimp with Keto Cauliflower Mash

Serves: 2 | Prep: 10 minutes | Cook : 20 minutes

Ingredients:

- 250g raw shrimp, peeled and deveined
- 2 tbsp unsalted butter (30g)
- 2 cloves garlic, minced
- 300g cauliflower florets
- 1 tbsp double cream (15ml)

Instructions:

1. Steam the cauliflower florets for 10-12 minutes until tender. Drain and mash with the double cream until smooth. Season with salt and pepper to taste.
2. In a large frying pan, melt the butter over medium heat. Add the minced garlic and cook for 1-2 minutes until fragrant.
3. Add the shrimp to the pan and cook for 3-4 minutes, or until pink and cooked through.
4. Serve the garlic butter shrimp with the cauliflower mash.

Chef's Tip: *For added flavour, sprinkle some grated Parmesan over the cauliflower mash before serving. You can also add a pinch of chilli flakes to the shrimp for a bit of heat.*

Nutritional Information (per serving):
- ✓ Calories: 340 kcal
- ✓ Fat: 25g
- ✓ Protein: 24g
- ✓ Carbohydrates: 4g

12. Keto Creamy Mussels with Sautéed Spinach

Serves: 2 | Prep: 10 minutes | Cook : 15 minutes

Ingredients:

- 500g mussels, cleaned
- 2 tbsp double cream (30ml)
- 1 tbsp unsalted butter (15g)
- 100g fresh spinach
- 1 clove garlic, minced

Instructions:

1. In a large saucepan, melt the butter over medium heat. Add the minced garlic and cook for 1-2 minutes until fragrant.
2. Add the mussels to the saucepan, cover, and cook for 5-7 minutes until the mussels open.
3. Stir in the double cream and cook for an additional 1-2 minutes until heated through.
4. In a separate pan, sauté the spinach over medium heat until wilted, about 3-4 minutes.
5. Serve the creamy mussels with the sautéed spinach on the side.

Chef's Tip: *For a bit of extra flavour, add a splash of white wine before covering the mussels. Discard any mussels that do not open.*

Nutritional Information (per serving):
- ✓ Calories: 310 kcal
- ✓ Fat: 22g
- ✓ Protein: 24g
- ✓ Carbohydrates: 4g

1. Zucchini Noodles with Alfredo Sauce

Serves: 2 | Prep: 10 minutes | Cook : 10 minutes

Ingredients:

- 2 medium courgettes (zucchini), spiralised (approx. 400g)
- 150 ml double cream
- 50g unsalted butter
- 60g grated Parmesan cheese
- 1/2 teaspoon sea salt

Instructions:

1. Heat a large frying pan over medium heat. Add the butter and let it melt completely.
2. Pour in the double cream and allow it to gently simmer for about 3-4 minutes, stirring frequently until it starts to thicken.
3. Stir in the grated Parmesan cheese and salt, mixing until smooth and creamy.
4. Add the spiralised courgettes to the sauce and cook for 2-3 minutes, tossing to coat, until the noodles are tender but still have some bite.
5. Serve immediately, garnished with extra Parmesan if desired.

Chef's Tip: *Courgettes are abundant in the UK, and using them as a pasta substitute keeps carbs low while adding fibre.*

Nutritional Information (per serving):
- ✓ Calories: 400 kcal
- ✓ Fat: 38g
- ✓ Protein: 9g
- ✓ Carbohydrates: 6g

2. Spaghetti Squash Carbonara

Serves: 2 | Prep: 10 minutes | Cook : 20 minutes

Ingredients:

- 1 small spaghetti squash (approx. 600g)
- 100g pancetta, diced
- 2 large egg yolks
- 50g grated Parmesan cheese
- 1 tablespoon olive oil

Instructions:

1. Preheat the oven to 200°C (180°C fan). Cut the spaghetti squash in half lengthwise, scoop out the seeds, and place the halves cut-side down on a baking tray. Bake for 20 minutes or until tender.
2. While the squash is baking, heat the olive oil in a frying pan over medium heat. Add the pancetta and cook until crispy, about 5-6 minutes.
3. In a bowl, whisk together the egg yolks and Parmesan cheese.
4. Once the squash is cooked, use a fork to scrape out the strands. Add the squash strands to the frying pan with the pancetta and mix well.
5. Remove the pan from the heat and quickly stir in the egg yolk mixture, tossing to coat evenly. Serve immediately.

Chef's Tip: *Spaghetti squash is a great low-carb alternative to pasta and is increasingly available in larger UK supermarkets.*

Nutritional Information (per serving):
- ✓ Calories: 320 kcal
- ✓ Fat: 26g
- ✓ Protein: 15g
- ✓ Carbohydrates: 9g

3. Cauliflower Risotto with Parmesan

Serves: 2 | Prep: 5 minutes | Cook : 15 minutes

Ingredients:

- 300g cauliflower, grated or riced
- 30g butter
- 100ml double cream
- 50g grated Parmesan cheese
- Salt and pepper, to taste

Instructions:

1.Heat the butter in a large frying pan over medium heat. Add the cauliflower rice and sauté for 5-6 minutes until tender.
2.Pour in the double cream and stir well. Let it simmer for 5 minutes until the mixture thickens.
3.Stir in the grated Parmesan cheese, and season with salt and pepper. Cook for another 2-3 minutes until creamy.
4.Serve warm as a side or main dish.

Chef's Tip: *Cauliflower rice is an easy and versatile substitute for rice and works wonderfully in creamy dishes like risotto.*

Nutritional Information (per serving):
- ✓ Calories: 280 kcal
- ✓ Fat: 24g
- ✓ Protein: 7g
- ✓ Carbohydrates: 5g

4. Cabbage Noodles with Bacon

Serves: 2 | Prep: 5 minutes | Cook : 15 minutes

Ingredients:

- 300g green cabbage, finely sliced
- 100g streaky bacon, diced
- 30g butter
- 1/2 teaspoon garlic powder
- Salt and pepper, to taste

Instructions:

1.Heat a large frying pan over medium heat. Add the diced bacon and cook until crispy, about 5-6 minutes.
2.Add the butter to the pan, then stir in the sliced cabbage and garlic powder. Cook for 8-10 minutes, stirring occasionally, until the cabbage is tender.
3.Season with salt and pepper to taste. Serve immediately.

Chef's Tip: *Cabbage is a budget-friendly vegetable that's low in carbs, making it a great option for keto meals.*

Nutritional Information (per serving):
- ✓ Calories: 220 kcal
- ✓ Fat: 20g
- ✓ Protein: 5g
- ✓ Carbohydrates: 5g

5. Cheesy Broccoli Stem Rice

Serves: 2 | Prep: 5 minutes | Cook : 10 minutes

Ingredients:

- 300 g broccoli stems
- 2 tbsp butter
- 75 g grated Cheddar cheese
- 1 tsp garlic powder
- Salt and black pepper to taste

Instructions:

1. Peel the tough outer layer of the broccoli stems and chop into small pieces. Pulse in a food processor until it resembles rice.
2. Heat the butter in a large pan over medium heat. Add the broccoli stem rice and sauté for 5-6 minutes until tender.
3. Stir in the garlic powder and grated Cheddar cheese, cooking until the cheese has melted and the mixture is creamy.
4. Season with salt and black pepper to taste. Serve as a side dish.

Chef's Tip: *Using broccoli stems reduces waste and makes for a tasty, low-carb alternative to traditional rice.*

Nutritional Information (per serving):
- ✓ Calories: 220 kcal
- ✓ Fat: 20g
- ✓ Protein: 6g
- ✓ Carbohydrates: 4g

6. Keto Faux Fried Rice with Egg

Serves: 2 | Prep: 5 minutes | Cook : 10 minutes

Ingredients:

- 300g cauliflower, grated or riced
- 2 large eggs, beaten
- 1 tablespoon coconut oil
- 1 tablespoon soy sauce (or tamari for gluten-free)
- 2 spring onions, chopped

Instructions:

1. Heat the coconut oil in a large frying pan or wok over medium heat. Add the cauliflower rice and stir-fry for 3-4 minutes until tender.
2. Push the cauliflower rice to one side of the pan and pour the beaten eggs into the empty side. Scramble the eggs until cooked through, then mix them with the cauliflower rice.
3. Add the soy sauce and chopped spring onions, stirring well to combine. Cook for an additional 1-2 minutes and serve immediately.

Chef's Tip: *Adding eggs to cauliflower rice boosts the protein content and gives this dish a more authentic fried rice texture.*

Nutritional Information (per serving):
- ✓ Calories: 180 kcal
- ✓ Fat: 13g
- ✓ Protein: 8g
- ✓ Carbohydrates: 5g

7. Keto Eggplant Lasagna Roll-Ups

Serves: 2 | Prep: 10 minutes | Cook : 20 minutes

Ingredients:

- 1 medium eggplant (approximately 250 g)
- 100 g ricotta cheese
- 50 g grated mozzarella
- 200 ml passata
- 1 tbsp olive oil

Instructions:

1.Preheat the oven to 200°C (180°C fan). Slice the eggplant lengthwise into thin strips (around 0.5 cm thick).
2.Heat the olive oil in a large pan over medium-high heat. Lightly cook the eggplant strips for 1-2 minutes per side, until softened.
3.Spread a thin layer of ricotta cheese onto each eggplant strip, then roll up and place seam-side down in a baking dish.
4.Pour the passata over the roll-ups and sprinkle with grated mozzarella.
5.Bake in the preheated oven for 15-20 minutes until the cheese is melted and bubbling. Serve warm.

Chef's Tip: *Substitute passata for crushed tomatoes if desired, adding a pinch of dried oregano for extra flavour.*

Nutritional Information (per serving):
- ✓ Calories: 210 kcal
- ✓ Fat: 16g
- ✓ Protein: 9g
- ✓ Carbohydrates: 8g

8. Zoodles with Creamy Avocado Sauce

Serves: 2 | Prep: 10 minutes | Cook : 5 minutes

Ingredients:

- 2 medium courgettes (approximately 300 g)
- 1 ripe avocado
- 2 tbsp extra virgin olive oil
- Juice of 1 lemon
- 1 clove garlic, minced

Instructions:

1.Use a spiralizer to create courgette noodles (zoodles). Alternatively, use a vegetable peeler to create thin ribbons.
2.In a food processor, blend the avocado, olive oil, lemon juice, and minced garlic until smooth. Season with salt and black pepper to taste.
3.Heat a large pan over medium heat and add the zoodles. Cook for 2-3 minutes until slightly tender.
4.Remove from heat and toss the zoodles with the creamy avocado sauce until well coated. Serve immediately.

Chef's Tip: *Avocado adds healthy fats to this dish, keeping it creamy and satisfying. Adjust the lemon juice to taste for extra zing.*

Nutritional Information (per serving):
- ✓ Calories: 250 kcal
- ✓ Fat: 22g
- ✓ Protein: 3g
- ✓ Carbohydrates: 8g

9. Mushroom & Herb Cauliflower Rice

Serves: 2 | Prep: 5 minutes | Cook : 10 minutes

Ingredients:

- 300 g cauliflower
- 150 g mushrooms, sliced
- 2 tbsp butter
- 1 tsp dried oregano
- 1 tbsp chopped fresh chives

Instructions:

1.Cut the cauliflower into florets and pulse in a food processor until it resembles rice.
2.Heat the butter in a large pan over medium heat. Add the mushrooms and sauté for 3-4 minutes until softened.
3.Add the cauliflower rice and dried oregano, cooking for another 5-6 minutes until tender.
4.Remove from heat and stir in the chopped chives.
Season with salt and black pepper to taste. Serve as a side dish.

Chef's Tip: *Mushrooms add an earthy flavour to this cauliflower rice, making it a perfect accompaniment to grilled meats or fish.*

Nutritional Information (per serving):
- ✓ Calories: 170 kcal
- ✓ Fat: 14g
- ✓ Protein: 4g
- ✓ Carbohydrates: 5g

10. Garlic-Parmesan Zucchini Noodle Salad

Serves: 2 | Prep: 10 minutes

Ingredients:

- 2 medium zucchinis (about 300 g), spiralized
- 50 g Parmesan cheese, grated
- 2 tablespoons extra virgin olive oil
- 1 garlic clove, minced
- 1/2 teaspoon sea salt

Instructions:

1.In a large bowl, combine the spiralized zucchini, grated Parmesan, olive oil, minced garlic, and sea salt.
2.Toss well to coat the zucchini noodles evenly.
3.Let the salad sit for 5-10 minutes to allow the flavours to meld together.
4.Serve immediately.

Chef's Tip: *Use freshly grated Parmesan for the best flavour. If you don't have a spiralizer, you can use a vegetable peeler to create thin ribbons.*

Nutritional Information (per serving):
- ✓ Calories: 220 kcal
- ✓ Fat: 18g
- ✓ Protein: 7g
- ✓ Carbohydrates: 6g

11. Spinach Pesto Shirataki Noodles

Serves: 2 | Prep: 5 minutes | Cook : 10 minutes

Ingredients:

- 200 g shirataki noodles
- 100 g fresh spinach
- 50 g pine nuts
- 50 ml extra virgin olive oil
- 30 g grated Parmesan cheese

Instructions:

1.Rinse the shirataki noodles under cold water for 2-3 minutes, then drain well and pat dry.
2.In a food processor, blend the spinach, pine nuts, olive oil, and Parmesan cheese until smooth. Season with salt and black pepper to taste.
3.Heat a large pan over medium heat and add the shirataki noodles. Cook for 2-3 minutes until heated through.
4.Remove from heat and toss the noodles with the spinach pesto until well coated. Serve immediately.

Chef's Tip: *Shirataki noodles are an excellent low-carb base for this fresh and vibrant pesto, keeping the dish light yet satisfying.*

Nutritional Information (per serving):

- ✓ Calories: 280 kcal
- ✓ Fat: 25g
- ✓ Protein: 5g
- ✓ Carbohydrates: 4g

12. Keto Mushroom Stroganoff over Zoodles

Serves: 2 | Prep: 10 minutes | Cook : 15 minutes

Ingredients:

- 200 g mushrooms, sliced
- 2 medium courgettes (approximately 300 g)
- 100 ml double cream
- 1 tbsp butter
- 1 tsp smoked paprika

Instructions:

1.Use a spiralizer to create courgette noodles (zoodles). Alternatively, use a vegetable peeler to create thin ribbons.
2.Heat the butter in a large pan over medium heat. Add the mushrooms and sauté for 5-6 minutes until softened.
3.Stir in the smoked paprika and double cream, cooking for another 3-4 minutes until the sauce is thickened.
4.In a separate pan, heat the zoodles for 2-3 minutes until slightly tender.
5.Serve the mushroom stroganoff over the zoodles. Season with salt and black pepper to taste.

Chef's Tip: *The smoked paprika adds depth to the creamy mushroom sauce, making it a comforting keto meal.*

Nutritional Information (per serving):

- ✓ Calories: 230 kcal
- ✓ Fat: 20g
- ✓ Protein: 4g
- ✓ Carbohydrates: 6g

1. Crispy Keto Cauliflower Tots

Serves: 4 | Prep: 10 minutes | Cook : 20 minutes

Ingredients:

- 300 g cauliflower florets
- 50 g almond flour
- 50 g mature cheddar cheese, grated
- 1 large egg
- 1/2 tsp onion powder

Instructions:

1. Preheat your oven to 200°C (180°C fan) and line a baking tray with parchment paper.
2. Steam the cauliflower florets until tender, about 5-7 minutes. Drain well and pat dry with a kitchen towel to remove excess moisture.
3. Mash the cauliflower in a bowl and mix in the almond flour, cheddar cheese, egg, and onion powder until well combined.
4. Form the mixture into small tot shapes and place them on the prepared baking tray.
5. Bake for 15-20 minutes, turning halfway, until golden and crispy.

Chef's Tip: *Almond flour keeps these tots low in carbs and adds a nutty flavour. Cauliflower is an excellent low-carb vegetable that fits well into a keto diet.*

Nutritional Information (per serving):

- ✓ Calories: 130 kcal
- ✓ Fat: 9g
- ✓ Protein: 6g
- ✓ Carbohydrates: 3g

2. Pepperoni Chips with Ranch Dip

Serves: 4 | Prep: 5 minutes | Cook : 10 minutes

Ingredients:

- 100 g pepperoni slices
- 100 ml sour cream
- 1/2 tsp dried dill
- 1/2 tsp dried parsley
- 1/4 tsp garlic powder

Instructions:

1. Preheat your oven to 200°C (180°C fan) and line a baking tray with parchment paper.
2. Place the pepperoni slices in a single layer on the baking tray.
3. Bake for 8-10 minutes, or until the pepperoni is crispy. Allow to cool on the tray.
4. In a small bowl, mix together the sour cream, dried dill, dried parsley, and garlic powder to make the ranch dip.
5. Serve the pepperoni chips with the ranch dip.

Chef's Tip: *Pepperoni makes a great low-carb snack, and pairing it with a high-fat dip like sour cream helps keep you in ketosis.*

Nutritional Information (per serving):

- ✓ Calories: 180 kcal
- ✓ Fat: 15g
- ✓ Protein: 7g
- ✓ Carbohydrates: 1g

3. Almond-Crusted Zucchini Fries

Serves: 4 | Prep: 10 minutes | Cook : 15 minutes

Ingredients:

- 2 medium zucchinis (about 300 g)
- 50 g almond flour
- 30 g grated parmesan cheese
- 1/2 tsp smoked paprika
- 1 large egg

Instructions:

1.Preheat your oven to 220°C (200°C fan) and line a baking tray with parchment paper.
2.Cut the zucchinis into fry-shaped sticks.
3.In a bowl, mix together the almond flour, parmesan cheese, and smoked paprika.
4.Beat the egg in a separate bowl. Dip each zucchini stick into the egg, then coat with the almond flour mixture.
5.Place the coated zucchini sticks on the prepared baking tray and bake for 15 minutes, or until golden and crispy.

Chef's Tip: *Almond flour adds healthy fats and keeps these fries low in carbs. These are perfect as a side dish or snack.*

Nutritional Information (per serving):
- ✓ Calories: 120 kcal
- ✓ Fat: 9g
- ✓ Protein: 5g
- ✓ Carbohydrates: 3g

4. Mini Sausage Pizza Bites

Serves: 4 | Prep: 10 minutes | Cook : 15 minutes

Ingredients:

- 8 mini pork sausages (about 200 g)
- 50 g tomato passata
- 50 g grated mozzarella cheese
- 1/2 tsp dried oregano
- 1/4 tsp garlic powder

Instructions:

1.Preheat your oven to 200°C (180°C fan) and line a baking tray with parchment paper.
2.Cook the mini sausages in a frying pan over medium heat until browned, about 5 minutes.
3.Place the sausages on the prepared baking tray and top each with a small amount of tomato passata.
4.Sprinkle grated mozzarella, dried oregano, and garlic powder over each sausage.
5.Bake for 10 minutes, or until the cheese is melted and bubbly.

Chef's Tip: *These pizza bites are a great keto-friendly snack or appetizer. Opt for high-quality sausages with minimal fillers for the best keto results.*

Nutritional Information (per serving):
- ✓ Calories: 190 kcal
- ✓ Fat: 15g
- ✓ Protein: 9g
- ✓ Carbohydrates: 2g

5. Spicy Pork Rind Nachos

Serves: 4 | Prep: 5 minutes | Cook : 5 minutes

Ingredients:

- 100 g pork rinds
- 50 g grated cheddar cheese
- 30 g sliced jalapeños
- 50 g sour cream
- 1/2 tsp smoked paprika

Instructions:

1.Preheat your oven to 200°C (180°C fan) and line a baking tray with parchment paper.
2.Spread the pork rinds on the baking tray and sprinkle with grated cheddar cheese and sliced jalapeños.
3.Bake for 5 minutes, or until the cheese is melted.
4.Remove from the oven, sprinkle with smoked paprika, and serve with sour cream on the side for dipping.

Chef's Tip: *Pork rinds are an excellent low-carb replacement for tortilla chips. Look for plain, unflavoured pork rinds to keep them keto-friendly.*

Nutritional Information (per serving):
- ✓ Calories: 220 kcal
- ✓ Fat: 18g
- ✓ Protein: 10g
- ✓ Carbohydrates: 1g

6. Crispy Parmesan Chicken Nuggets

Serves: 4 | Prep: 10 minutes | Cook : 15 minutes

Ingredients:

- 300 g chicken breast, cut into bite-sized pieces
- 50 g grated parmesan cheese
- 50 g almond flour
- 1/2 tsp smoked paprika
- 1 large egg

Instructions:

1.Preheat your oven to 200°C (180°C fan) and line a baking tray with parchment paper.
2.In a bowl, mix together the parmesan, almond flour, and smoked paprika.
3.Beat the egg in a separate bowl. Dip each chicken piece into the egg, then coat with the parmesan mixture.
4.Place the coated chicken pieces on the prepared baking tray and bake for 15 minutes, or until golden and cooked through.

Chef's Tip: *These nuggets are perfect for dipping in a keto-friendly sauce. Almond flour keeps them low in carbs while adding healthy fats.*

Nutritional Information (per serving):
- ✓ Calories: 180 kcal
- ✓ Fat: 11g
- ✓ Protein: 18g
- ✓ Carbohydrates: 2g

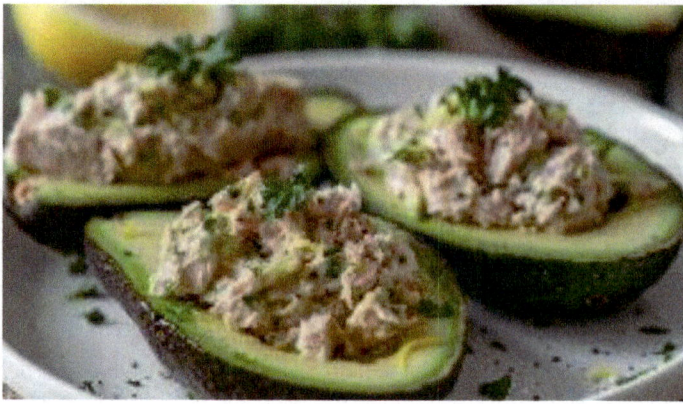

7. Avocado Tuna Boats

Serves: 4 | Prep: 5 minutes | Cook : 0 minutes

Ingredients:

- 2 ripe avocados
- 150 g tinned tuna in olive oil, drained
- 2 tbsp mayonnaise
- 1/2 tsp lemon juice
- Pinch of sea salt and black pepper

Instructions:

1. Cut the avocados in half and remove the pits.
2. In a bowl, mix together the tuna, mayonnaise, lemon juice, salt, and pepper.
3. Spoon the tuna mixture into the avocado halves, dividing it evenly.
4. Serve immediately.

Chef's Tip: *Avocados are rich in healthy fats, making them perfect for keto. The tuna adds protein and omega-3s, keeping you satisfied longer.*

Nutritional Information (per serving):

- ✓ Calories: 210 kcal
- ✓ Fat: 18g
- ✓ Protein: 9g
- ✓ Carbohydrates: 3g

8. Crispy Bacon-Wrapped Brussels Sprouts

Serves: 4 | Prep: 10 minutes | Cook : 20 minutes

Ingredients:

- 12 Brussels sprouts (around 300g)
- 8 rashers streaky bacon
- 1 tablespoon olive oil (15ml)
- 1/2 teaspoon black pepper
- 1/2 teaspoon paprika

Instructions:

1. Preheat your oven to 200°C (180°C fan/gas mark 6).
2. Trim the Brussels sprouts by removing any tough outer leaves and slicing the stalk end off.
3. Wrap each Brussels sprout in half a rasher of streaky bacon and secure with a cocktail stick if necessary.
4. Place the bacon-wrapped sprouts on a baking tray and drizzle with olive oil. Sprinkle with black pepper and paprika.
5. Bake in the oven for 20 minutes, turning halfway through, until the bacon is crispy and the sprouts are tender.

Chef's Tip: *Swap Brussels sprouts for broccoli florets if desired. Bacon is rich in fats while Brussels sprouts keep the carbs low—a great way to stay on track.*

Nutritional Information (per serving):

- ✓ Calories: 150 kcal
- ✓ Fat: 12g
- ✓ Protein: 6g
- ✓ Carbohydrates: 3g

9. Keto Garlic Parmesan Shrimp Skewers

Serves: 2 | Prep: 10 minutes | Cook : 10 minutes

Ingredients:

- 300g raw shrimp (peeled and deveined)
- 2 tablespoons grated Parmesan cheese (15g)
- 2 tablespoons melted butter (30g)
- 2 cloves garlic, minced
- 1 tablespoon lemon juice (15ml)

Instructions:

1.Preheat your grill to medium-high heat or prepare a grill pan.
2.In a bowl, mix melted butter, garlic, and lemon juice.
3.Thread the shrimp onto skewers, brush with the butter mixture, and sprinkle with grated Parmesan.
4.Place skewers on the grill and cook for 3-4 minutes per side or until shrimp turn pink and are fully cooked.
5.Serve hot with any extra garlic butter drizzled on top.

Chef's Tip: *Use jumbo prawns, which are often easier to find in the UK and are perfect for grilling. The fats from butter and cheese help you stay in ketosis.*

Nutritional Information (per serving):
- ✓ Calories: 240 kcal
- ✓ Fat: 18g
- ✓ Protein: 18g
- ✓ Carbohydrates: 1g

10. Keto Guacamole-Stuffed Mini Peppers

Serves: 4 | Prep: 10 minutes | Cook : None

Ingredients:

- 8 mini sweet peppers (200g)
- 1 ripe avocado (150g)
- Juice of 1 lime (15ml)
- 1/4 teaspoon garlic powder
- 1/4 teaspoon sea salt

Instructions:

1.Cut the tops off the mini peppers and remove any seeds.
2.In a bowl, mash the avocado with lime juice, garlic powder, and sea salt until smooth.
3.Stuff each mini pepper with the guacamole mixture.
4.Serve immediately or refrigerate until ready to eat..

Chef's Tip: *Mini sweet peppers are readily available in UK supermarkets and make a great crunchy vessel for the creamy, high-fat guacamole, which supports ketosis perfectly.*

Nutritional Information (per serving):
- ✓ Calories: 100 kcal
- ✓ Fat: 8g
- ✓ Protein: 1g
- ✓ Carbohydrates: 4g

11. Cucumber Bites with Smoked Salmon & Cream Cheese

Serves: 4 | Prep: 10 minutes | Cook : None

Ingredients:

- 1 cucumber (approx. 300g)
- 100g smoked salmon
- 100g cream cheese
- 1 tablespoon lemon juice (15ml)
- 1/4 teaspoon black pepper

Instructions:

1. Slice the cucumber into 1cm thick rounds.
2. Spread a small amount of cream cheese on each cucumber slice.
3. Top each slice with a piece of smoked salmon.
4. Drizzle with lemon juice and sprinkle with black pepper.
5. Serve immediately or refrigerate until ready to serve.

Chef's Tip: *Smoked salmon is high in healthy fats, making it ideal for keto. You can also use smoked mackerel as an alternative.*

Nutritional Information (per serving):
- ✓ Calories: 120 kcal
- ✓ Fat: 10g
- ✓ Protein: 6g
- ✓ Carbohydrates: 2g

12. Crispy Keto Eggplant Fries

Serves: 2 | Prep: 10 minutes | Cook : 15 minutes

Ingredients:

- 1 medium eggplant (approx. 300g)
- 2 tablespoons olive oil (30ml)
- 1 tablespoon grated Parmesan cheese (8g)
- 1/2 teaspoon paprika
- 1/2 teaspoon sea salt

Instructions:

1. Preheat the oven to 200°C (180°C fan/gas mark 6).
2. Slice the eggplant into fry-like strips.
3. In a bowl, mix the olive oil, Parmesan cheese, paprika, and sea salt.
4. Toss the eggplant strips in the mixture until evenly coated.
5. Place the strips on a baking tray lined with parchment paper and bake for 15 minutes, turning halfway through, until crispy.

Chef's Tip: *Eggplant is a great low-carb substitute for potatoes. The Parmesan adds flavour and helps to crisp the fries.*

Nutritional Information (per serving):
- ✓ Calories: 140 kcal
- ✓ Fat: 12g
- ✓ Protein: 3g
- ✓ Carbohydrates: 4g

13. Keto Pesto Mozzarella Skewers

Serves: 4 | Prep: 10 minutes | Cook : None

Ingredients:

- 200g mozzarella balls
- 100g cherry tomatoes
- 2 tablespoons pesto (30g)
- 1 tablespoon olive oil (15ml)
- 8 fresh basil leaves

Instructions:

1. Thread the mozzarella balls, cherry tomatoes, and basil leaves onto skewers.
2. In a small bowl, mix the pesto with olive oil.
3. Drizzle the pesto mixture over the skewers.
4. Serve immediately or refrigerate until ready to eat.

Chef's Tip: *Use fresh mozzarella for the best flavour. The pesto adds healthy fats and a burst of flavour.*

Nutritional Information (per serving):

- ✓ Calories: 170 kcal
- ✓ Fat: 14g
- ✓ Protein: 7g
- ✓ Carbohydrates: 2g

14. Low-Carb Ham and Cheese Roll-Ups

Serves: 2 | Prep: 5 minutes | Cook : None

Ingredients:

- 4 slices cooked ham (100g)
- 4 slices cheddar cheese (80g)
- 1 tablespoon wholegrain mustard (15g)
- 1 tablespoon mayonnaise (15g)

Instructions:

1. Lay the ham slices flat and spread a small amount of wholegrain mustard and mayonnaise on each.
2. Place a slice of cheddar cheese on each ham slice.
3. Roll each ham slice tightly to create roll-ups.
4. Cut in half and serve immediately or refrigerate.

Chef's Tip: *Use cooked ham from the deli counter for convenience. The combination of cheese and mayonnaise ensures high fat content, perfect for keto.*

Nutritional Information (per serving):

- ✓ Calories: 200 kcal
- ✓ Fat: 16g
- ✓ Protein: 12g
- ✓ Carbohydrates: 1g

15. Zucchini and Cream Cheese Roll-Ups

Serves: 4 | Prep: 10 minutes | Cook : None

Ingredients:

- 1 large zucchini (approx. 300g)
- 100g cream cheese
- 50g smoked ham
- 1 tablespoon fresh dill, chopped
- 1/4 teaspoon sea salt

Instructions:

1. Use a vegetable peeler to slice the zucchini lengthwise into thin strips.
2. Spread a small amount of cream cheese on each strip of zucchini.
3. Place a small piece of smoked ham on top and sprinkle with chopped dill.
4. Roll up each strip tightly and secure with a cocktail stick if necessary.
5. Sprinkle with sea salt and serve immediately or refrigerate until ready.

Chef's Tip: *Zucchini is a great low-carb substitute for wraps. The cream cheese provides fats to keep you in ketosis.*

Nutritional Information (per serving):
- ✓ Calories: 120 kcal
- ✓ Fat: 10g
- ✓ Protein: 4g
- ✓ Carbohydrates: 2g

16. Keto Herb-Marinated Olives

Serves: 4 | Prep: 5 minutes | Chill for 1 hour

Ingredients:

- 200g mixed olives
- 2 tablespoons olive oil (30ml)
- 1 tablespoon lemon zest
- 1 teaspoon dried oregano
- 1/2 teaspoon crushed red pepper flakes

Instructions:

1. In a bowl, combine the olive oil, lemon zest, oregano, and crushed red pepper flakes.
2. Add the olives and mix until well coated.
3. Transfer to an airtight container and let marinate in the fridge for at least 1 hour before serving.

Chef's Tip: *Marinated olives are a perfect high-fat keto snack. Use a mix of green and black olives for variety.*

Nutritional Information (per serving):
- ✓ Calories: 110 kcal
- ✓ Fat: 11g
- ✓ Protein: 1g
- ✓ Carbohydrates: 1g

1. Chocolate Avocado Mousse

Serves: 2 | Prep: 5 minutes | Cook : None

Ingredients:

- 1 large ripe avocado (approx. 150g)
- 25g unsweetened cocoa powder
- 60ml double cream
- 2 tbsp powdered erythritol (or to taste)
- 1/2 tsp vanilla extract

Instructions:

1. Cut the avocado in half, remove the pit, and scoop the flesh into a food processor.
2. Add the cocoa powder, double cream, powdered erythritol, and vanilla extract.
3. Blend until smooth and creamy. Taste and adjust sweetness if necessary.
4. Transfer to serving bowls and chill in the fridge for 10 minutes before serving.

Chef's Tip: *Keep a few avocados on hand as they're versatile for keto recipes. Substitute erythritol with stevia if preferred.*

Nutritional Information (per serving):

✓ Calories: 247 kcal
✓ Fat: 24g
✓ Protein: 3g
✓ Carbohydrates: 5g

2. Peanut Butter Fat Bombs

Serves: 8 | Prep: 10 minutes | (chill for 30 minutes)

Ingredients:

- 120g natural peanut butter (no added sugar)
- 60g coconut oil
- 2 tbsp powdered erythritol
- 1/2 tsp vanilla extract
- Pinch of sea salt

Instructions:

1. In a small bowl, combine peanut butter, coconut oil, powdered erythritol, vanilla extract, and salt.
2. Mix well until smooth and combined.
3. Spoon the mixture into silicone moulds or an ice cube tray, filling each section about three-quarters full.
4. Freeze for at least 30 minutes or until solid.
5. Pop out the fat bombs and store in an airtight container in the fridge.

Chef's Tip: *Opt for UK-sourced peanut butter with no added sugar. These fat bombs are perfect for curbing cravings between meals.*

Nutritional Information (per serving):

✓ Calories: 134 kcal
✓ Fat: 14g
✓ Protein: 2g
✓ Carbohydrates: 1g

3. Raspberry Almond Tarts

Serves: 4 | Prep: 10 minutes | Cook : 15 minutes

Ingredients:

- 100g almond flour
- 50g unsalted butter, melted
- 2 tbsp powdered erythritol
- 60g fresh raspberries
- 1/2 tsp vanilla extract

Instructions:

1. Preheat your oven to 180°C (fan 160°C) and grease four tartlet tins.
2. In a bowl, mix almond flour, melted butter, erythritol, and vanilla extract until combined.
3. Press the mixture into the tartlet tins to form crusts. Place a few raspberries in each tartlet.
4. Bake for 15 minutes or until the crust is golden. Let cool before serving.

Chef's Tip: *For a twist, substitute raspberries with blackberries. Almond flour is a keto pantry staple in the UK for creating quick, low-carb bases.*

Nutritional Information (per serving):
- ✓ Calories: 168 kcal
- ✓ Fat: 15g
- ✓ Protein: 3g
- ✓ Carbohydrates: 4g

4. Coconut Macaroons with Dark Chocolate

Serves: 6 | Prep: 10 minutes | Cook : 15 minutes

Ingredients:

- 100g desiccated coconut
- 2 large egg whites
- 2 tbsp powdered erythritol
- 1/2 tsp vanilla extract
- 50g dark chocolate (85% cocoa or higher), melted

Instructions:

1. Preheat your oven to 180°C (fan 160°C) and line a baking tray with parchment paper.
2. In a mixing bowl, combine desiccated coconut, egg whites, erythritol, and vanilla extract.
3. Scoop tablespoon-sized portions of the mixture onto the baking tray, forming small mounds.
4. Bake for 15 minutes or until golden brown. Let cool completely.
5. Drizzle the melted dark chocolate over the cooled macaroons and let set before serving.

Chef's Tip: *Desiccated coconut is widely available in the UK and adds healthy fats to your diet.*

Nutritional Information (per serving):
- ✓ Calories: 130 kcal
- ✓ Fat: 11g
- ✓ Protein: 2g
- ✓ Carbohydrates: 4g

5. Keto Vanilla Custard Cups

Serves: 4 | Prep: 5 minutes | Cook : 20 minutes

Ingredients:

- 200ml double cream
- 2 large egg yolks
- 1 tbsp powdered erythritol
- 1/2 tsp vanilla extract
- Pinch of sea salt

Instructions:

1. Preheat your oven to 160°C (fan 140°C). Place four ramekins in a baking dish.
2. In a saucepan, heat the double cream over low heat until just simmering.
3. In a mixing bowl, whisk the egg yolks, erythritol, vanilla extract, and salt.
4. Slowly pour the heated cream into the egg mixture while whisking continuously.
5. Pour the mixture into the ramekins. Fill the baking dish with hot water until it reaches halfway up the sides of the ramekins.

Chef's Tip: *Double cream is an excellent source of fat for keto diets and is readily available in UK supermarkets.*

Nutritional Information (per serving):
- ✓ Calories: 180 kcal
- ✓ Fat: 18g
- ✓ Protein: 3g
- ✓ Carbohydrates: 1g

6. Almond Butter Brownies

Serves: 6 | Prep: 10 minutes | Cook : 20 minutes

Ingredients:

- 150g almond butter
- 1 large egg
- 2 tbsp powdered erythritol
- 1/2 tsp baking powder
- 25g unsweetened cocoa powder

Instructions:

1. Preheat your oven to 180°C (fan 160°C) and line a small baking dish with parchment paper.
2. In a mixing bowl, combine almond butter, egg, erythritol, baking powder, and cocoa powder until smooth.
3. Pour the mixture into the prepared baking dish and spread evenly.
4. Bake for 20 minutes or until a toothpick inserted in the centre comes out clean.
5. Let cool before slicing into squares.

Chef's Tip: *Almond butter can be substituted with hazelnut butter for a different flavour profile.*

Nutritional Information (per serving):
- ✓ Calories: 190 kcal
- ✓ Fat: 16g
- ✓ Protein: 5g
- ✓ Carbohydrates: 3g

7. Strawberry Cream Popsicles

Serves: 4 | Prep: 5 minutes |
Cook : 0 minutes (freeze for 4 hours)

Ingredients:

- 100g fresh strawberries
- 100ml double cream
- 2 tbsp powdered erythritol
- 50g Greek yoghurt
- 1/2 tsp vanilla extract

Instructions:

1.In a blender, combine strawberries, double cream, erythritol, Greek yoghurt, and vanilla extract. Blend until smooth.
2.Pour the mixture into popsicle moulds and insert sticks.
3.Freeze for at least 4 hours or until solid.
4.Remove from the moulds and enjoy.

Chef's Tip: *For a creamier texture, use full-fat Greek yoghurt. Strawberries can be substituted with raspberries for a tart flavour.*

Nutritional Information (per serving):
- ✓ Calories: 98 kcal
- ✓ Fat: 8g
- ✓ Protein: 2g
- ✓ Carbohydrates: 3g

8. Keto Chocolate Chip Cookies

Serves: 8 | Prep: 10 minutes | Cook : 12 minutes

Ingredients:

- 100g almond flour
- 50g unsalted butter, melted
- 2 tbsp powdered erythritol
- 1/2 tsp vanilla extract
- 40g sugar-free dark chocolate chips

Instructions:

1.Preheat your oven to 180°C (fan 160°C) and line a baking tray with parchment paper.
2.In a bowl, combine almond flour, melted butter, erythritol, and vanilla extract. Mix until a dough forms.
3.Fold in the dark chocolate chips.
4.Scoop tablespoon-sized portions of the dough onto the baking tray, flattening them slightly.
5.Bake for 10-12 minutes or until the edges are golden brown. Let cool before serving.

Chef's Tip: *Dark chocolate chips with at least 85% cocoa are recommended to keep sugar content low.*

Nutritional Information (per serving):
- ✓ Calories: 122 kcal
- ✓ Fat: 11g
- ✓ Protein: 3g
- ✓ Carbohydrates: 2g

9. Keto Peanut Butter Blondies

Serves: 6 | Prep: 10 minutes | Cook : 20 minutes

Ingredients:

- 150g natural peanut butter (no added sugar)
- 1 large egg
- 2 tbsp powdered erythritol
- 1/2 tsp baking powder
- 1/2 tsp vanilla extract

Instructions:

1. Preheat your oven to 180°C (fan 160°C) and line a small baking dish with parchment paper.
2. In a mixing bowl, combine peanut butter, egg, erythritol, baking powder, and vanilla extract. Mix until smooth.
3. Pour the mixture into the prepared baking dish and spread evenly.
4. Bake for 20 minutes or until a toothpick inserted in the centre comes out clean.
5. Let cool before slicing into squares.

Chef's Tip: *Natural peanut butter without added sugar is ideal for keeping net carbs low*

Nutritional Information (per serving):

- ✓ Calories: 175 kcal
- ✓ Fat: 14g
- ✓ Protein: 5g
- ✓ Carbohydrates: 2g

10. Creamy Keto Coconut Panna Cotta

Serves: 4 | Prep: 10 minutes | Cook : 20 minutes (plus 2 hours chilling time)

Ingredients:

- 400 ml full-fat coconut milk
- 250 ml double cream
- 1 tbsp powdered gelatin
- 2 tbsp erythritol (or sweetener of choice)
- 1 tsp vanilla extract

Instructions:

1. In a saucepan, combine the coconut milk, double cream, and erythritol. Heat over medium heat until the mixture begins to steam, but do not let it boil.
2. Sprinkle the gelatin evenly over the mixture while whisking continuously to prevent lumps. Stir until the gelatin is completely dissolved.
3. Add the vanilla extract and stir until well combined.
4. Pour the mixture evenly into four serving ramekins and let them cool for about 10 minutes.
5. Transfer to the fridge and chill for at least 2 hours or until set.
6. To serve, optionally garnish with fresh berries (keeping the carb count in mind).

Chef's Tip: *Make sure to use a sweetener like erythritol that does not affect blood sugar levels, which is important for staying in ketosis. UK coconut milk brands like Blue Dragon are recommended.*

Nutritional Information (per serving):

- ✓ Calories: 330 kcal
- ✓ Fat: 33g
- ✓ Protein: 3g
- ✓ Carbohydrates: 2g

11. No-Bake Keto Berry Cheesecake Bites

Serves: 8 | Prep: 15 minutes | Chill Time: 2 hours

Ingredients:

- 200 g full-fat cream cheese
- 100 g mixed berries (raspberries, blueberries, or strawberries)
- 3 tbsp powdered erythritol
- 50 g unsalted butter
- 100 g almond flour

Instructions:

1. In a bowl, mix almond flour and melted butter until well combined. Press the mixture into the bottom of a lined 20 cm square dish to form a crust.
2. In another bowl, mix the cream cheese and erythritol until smooth and creamy.
3. Spread the cream cheese mixture evenly over the crust.
4. Scatter the mixed berries on top, pressing them lightly into the cream cheese.
5. Chill in the fridge for 2 hours, then cut into bite-sized pieces to serve.

Chef's Tip: *For UK audiences, try sourcing cream cheese like Philadelphia or similar brands. Use locally available berries for freshness and better flavour.*

Nutritional Information (per serving):
- ✓ Calories: 165 kcal
- ✓ Fat: 15g
- ✓ Protein: 3g
- ✓ Carbohydrates: 2g

12. Coconut Lime Keto Bliss Balls

Serves: 12 | Prep: 10 minutes | Chill Time: 1 hour

Ingredients:

- 100 g desiccated coconut
- 50 g almond flour
- 50 g coconut oil, melted
- 1 tbsp powdered erythritol
- 1 tbsp lime zest

Instructions:

1. In a bowl, mix the desiccated coconut, almond flour, erythritol, and lime zest until well combined.
2. Add the melted coconut oil and mix until the mixture sticks together.
3. Shape into small balls and place onto a parchment-lined tray.
4. Chill in the fridge for at least 1 hour until firm.
5. Serve as a tangy, high-fat treat.

Chef's Tip: *Lime zest adds a refreshing twist to the coconut flavour. Make sure to use unwaxed limes for zesting.*

Nutritional Information (per serving):
- ✓ Calories: 90 kcal
- ✓ Fat: 9g
- ✓ Protein: 1g
- ✓ Carbohydrates: 1g

1.Classic Keto Hollandaise Sauce

Serves: 4 servings | Prep Time: 5 minutes | Cook Time: 10 minutes

Ingredients:

- 3 large egg yolks
- 150 g unsalted butter
- 1 tbsp lemon juice
- 1/2 tsp Dijon mustard
- Pinch of sea salt

Use free-range eggs and high-quality butter for a richer flavour. This sauce is perfect to pair with eggs Benedict or any keto breakfast to enhance your fat intake.

Instructions:

1.Melt the butter in a small saucepan over low heat until fully melted. Make sure not to brown the butter.
2.In a heatproof bowl, whisk together the egg yolks, lemon juice, Dijon mustard, and a pinch of sea salt.
3.Place the bowl over a saucepan with gently simmering water, creating a double boiler. Continue whisking constantly until the mixture starts to thicken.
4.Slowly pour in the melted butter, whisking continuously until the sauce becomes creamy and thick.
5.Remove from heat, taste, and adjust salt or lemon juice as needed. Serve immediately over poached eggs, steamed asparagus, or grilled salmon.

Nutritional Information (per serving): **Calories: 210 kcal • Protein: 3g • Carbohydrates: 0,4g • Fats: 23g**

2.Creamy Garlic Alfredo Sauce

Serves: 4 servings | Prep Time: 5 minutes | Cook Time: 15 minutes

Ingredients:

- 100 g unsalted butter
- 100 ml double cream
- 3 cloves garlic, minced
- 50 g grated Parmesan cheese
- Pinch of black pepper

For a nutty twisttry using grated Pecorino Romano cheese instead of Parmesan. This sauce is also excellent for adding creamy texture to chicken dishes.

Instructions:

1.In a medium saucepan over medium heat, melt the butter and add the minced garlic. Cook for 1-2 minutes until the garlic becomes fragrant.
2.Reduce heat to low, and stir in the double cream. Cook for another 3-4 minutes, ensuring the mixture does not boil.
3.Add the grated Parmesan cheese gradually, stirring constantly until the cheese is fully melted and the sauce is smooth.
4.Season with black pepper and cook for another 1-2 minutes until thickened. Serve over steamed vegetables or zoodles.

Nutritional Information (per serving): **Calories: 260 kcal • Protein: 5g • Carbohydrates: 1g • Fats: 27g**

3.Spicy Chipotle Mayo

Serves: 4 servings | Prep Time: 5 minutes

Ingredients:

- 120 ml mayonnaise (full fat)
- 1 tbsp chipotle paste
- Juice of 1/2 lime
- 1/4 tsp smoked paprika
- Pinch of sea salt

For extra heat, add a pinch of cayenne pepper. This mayo can be stored in an airtight container in the fridge for up to 1 week.

Instructions:

1.In a medium bowl, combine the mayonnaise, chipotle paste, lime juice, smoked paprika, and sea salt.
2.Stir until all ingredients are well combined and the mixture is smooth.
3.Use as a dip for keto-friendly fries, as a spread for burgers, or to spice up any keto meal.

Nutritional Information (per serving): **Calories: 120 kcal • Protein: 0,2g • Carbohydrates: 0,5g • Fats: 13g**

4. Zesty Lemon Butter Sauce

Serves: 4 servings | Prep Time: 3 minutes | Cook Time: 5 minutes

Ingredients:

- 100 g unsalted butter
- Juice of 1 lemon
- 1 tsp lemon zest
- 1/2 tsp sea salt
- 1/4 tsp ground black pepper

Use organic lemons for a fresh, vibrant taste. This sauce works beautifully with seafood, especially salmon or cod.

Instructions:

1. In a small saucepan over low heat, melt the butter.
2. Stir in the lemon juice, lemon zest, sea salt, and black pepper.
3. Cook for 2-3 minutes, stirring occasionally, until all ingredients are well combined.
4. Drizzle over grilled fish, chicken, or steamed vegetables.

Nutritional Information (per serving): **Calories:** 140 kcal • **Protein:** 0,2g • **Carbohydrates:** 0,5g • **Fats:** 15g

5. 5-Minute Creamy Pesto Sauce

Serves: 4 servings | Prep Time: 5 minutes

Ingredients:

- 50 g fresh basil leaves
- 60 g grated Parmesan cheese
- 100 ml extra virgin olive oil
- 30 g pine nuts
- 1/2 tsp sea salt

Store any leftover pesto in an airtight container in the fridge for up to 3 days. To keep it fresh, add a thin layer of olive oil on top.

Instructions:

1. In a blender or food processor, combine the basil leaves, grated Parmesan cheese, pine nuts, and sea salt.
2. Pulse until the ingredients are roughly chopped.
3. Gradually add the olive oil while blending until a smooth, creamy consistency is achieved.
4. Use immediately as a sauce for zoodles, grilled chicken, or vegetables.

Nutritional Information (per serving): **Calories:** 200 kcal • **Protein:** 4g • **Carbohydrates:** 1g • **Fats:** 21g

6. Classic Keto Marinara Sauce

Serves: 4 servings | Prep Time: 5 minutes | Cook Time: 20 minutes

Ingredients:

- 400 g tinned chopped tomatoes
- 2 cloves garlic, minced
- 2 tbsp extra virgin olive oil
- 1/2 tsp dried oregano
- 1/2 tsp sea salt

For added flavour, stir in a few fresh basil leaves before serving. This sauce can be stored in the fridge for up to 5 days.

Instructions:

1. In a medium saucepan over medium heat, heat the olive oil and add the minced garlic. Sauté for 1-2 minutes until fragrant.
2. Add the tinned chopped tomatoes, dried oregano, and sea salt. Stir to combine.
3. Reduce heat to low and simmer for 15-20 minutes, stirring occasionally, until the sauce has thickened.
4. Use as a sauce for keto-friendly pasta alternatives or as a base for keto pizzas.

Nutritional Information (per serving): **Calories:** 70 kcal • **Protein:** 1g • **Carbohydrates:** 3g • **Fats:** 7g

7. Roasted Red Pepper Sauce

Serves: 4 servings | Prep Time: 5 minutes | Cook Time: 10 minutes

Ingredients:

- 2 large red bell peppers
- 60 ml extra virgin olive oil
- 1 clove garlic, minced
- 1/2 tsp smoked paprika
- Pinch of sea salt

For a spicy kick, add a pinch of chilli flakes. This sauce can be stored in the fridge for up to 3 days.

Instructions:

1. Preheat the oven to 200°C (180°C fan). Place the red bell peppers on a baking tray and roast for 10 minutes or until the skins are blistered.
2. Remove the peppers from the oven, allow to cool slightly, then peel off the skins and remove the seeds.
3. In a blender, combine the roasted peppers, olive oil, minced garlic, smoked paprika, and sea salt. Blend until smooth.
4. Use as a sauce for grilled meats, vegetables, or as a dip.

Nutritional Information (per serving): **Calories:** 90 kcal • **Protein:** 0,5g • **Carbohydrates:** 2g • **Fats:** 9g

8. Smoky Paprika Aioli

Serves: 4 servings | Prep Time: 5 minutes

Ingredients:

- 120 ml mayonnaise (full fat)
- 1 clove garlic, minced
- 1 tsp smoked paprika
- 1/2 tsp lemon juice
- Pinch of sea salt

For extra smokiness, add an additional 1/2 tsp of smoked paprika. This aioli can be stored in the fridge for up to 1 week.

Instructions:

1. In a medium bowl, combine the mayonnaise, minced garlic, smoked paprika, lemon juice, and sea salt.
2. Stir until smooth and well combined.
3. Use as a dip for vegetables, spread for burgers, or topping for grilled meats.

Nutritional Information (per serving): **Calories:** 130 kcal • **Protein:** 0,2g • **Carbohydrates:** 0,5g • **Fats:** 14g

9. Dairy-Free Cashew Cream Sauce

Serves: 4 servings | Prep Time: 5 minutes (plus soaking time) | Cook Time: 5 minutes

Ingredients:

- 150 g raw cashews (soaked in water for at least 2 hours)
- 120 ml water
- 1 tbsp lemon juice
- 1/2 tsp garlic powder
- Pinch of sea salt

This sauce can be stored in the fridge for up to 3 days. For extra flavour, add a pinch of nutritional yeast.

Instructions:

1. Drain and rinse the soaked cashews.
2. In a blender, combine the cashews, water, lemon juice, garlic powder, and sea salt.
3. Blend until smooth and creamy, adding more water if necessary to reach the desired consistency.
4. Use as a dairy-free alternative to cream sauces, perfect for pasta, vegetables, or as a dip.

Nutritional Information (per serving): **Calories:** 130 kcal • **Protein:** 4g • **Carbohydrates:** 6g • **Fats:** 10g

10. Herb Butter Sauce for Steak

Serves: 4 servings | Prep Time: 3 minutes | Cook Time: 5 minutes

Ingredients:

- 100 g unsalted butter
- 1 tbsp fresh parsley, chopped
- 1 tsp fresh thyme leaves
- 1/2 tsp garlic powder
- Pinch of sea salt

This sauce pairs wonderfully with ribeye or sirloin steak. For a richer flavour, add a splash of Worcestershire sauce.

Instructions:

1. In a small saucepan over low heat, melt the butter.
2. Stir in the chopped parsley, thyme, garlic powder, and sea salt.
3. Cook for 2-3 minutes, allowing the herbs to infuse the butter.
4. Drizzle over cooked steak or grilled meats.

Nutritional Information (per serving): **Calories: 130 kcal • Protein: 0,2g • Carbohydrates: 0,5g • Fats: 14g**

11. Coconut Curry Sauce

Serves: 4 servings | Prep Time: 5 minutes | Cook Time: 10 minutes

Ingredients:

- 200 ml coconut milk (full fat)
- 1 tbsp red curry paste
- 1/2 tsp ground turmeric
- 1/2 tsp sea salt
- 1/4 tsp ground black pepper

For extra spice, add a pinch of chilli flakes. This sauce works particularly well with prawns or cauliflower.

Instructions:

1. In a medium saucepan over medium heat, combine the coconut milk, red curry paste, ground turmeric, sea salt, and black pepper.
2. Stir well and bring to a gentle simmer.
3. Cook for 8-10 minutes, stirring occasionally, until the sauce has thickened.
4. Use as a sauce for chicken, vegetables, or fish.

Nutritional Information (per serving): **Calories: 150 kcal • Protein: 1g • Carbohydrates: 3g • Fats: 15g**

12. Cheddar Cheese Sauce

Serves: 4 servings | Prep Time: 5 minutes | Cook Time: 10 minutes

Ingredients:

- 100 g grated Cheddar cheese
- 100 ml double cream
- 20 g unsalted butter
- 1/2 tsp mustard powder
- Pinch of sea salt

For a smokier flavour, ue smoked Cheddar cheese. This sauce is ideal for cauliflower or broccoli.

Instructions:

1. In a medium saucepan over low heat, melt the butter and stir in the double cream.
2. Gradually add the grated Cheddar cheese, stirring continuously until melted and smooth.
3. Stir in the mustard powder and sea salt, cooking for another 1-2 minutes until thickened.
4. Serve over steamed vegetables, grilled meats, or use as a dip.

Nutritional Information (per serving): **Calories: 180 kcal • Protein: 5g • Carbohydrates: 1g • Fats: 18g**

30 – Days Meal Plan

Day	Breakfast	Lunch	Snack	Dinner	Kcal
Day 1	Smoked Salmon and Dill Egg Bites (3 egg bites) p.12	Keto Chicken Alfredo Bake p.35 + Spicy Cabbage Slaw with Jalapeño p.30	Low-Carb Ham and Cheese Roll-Ups (2 servings) p.67	Garlic Butter Chicken Bites with Broccoli p.38	1560
Day 2	Pepperoni and Cheese Egg Cups p.14	Creamy Broccoli Cheddar Soup p.23	Keto Pesto Mozzarella Skewers p.67	Keto Pork Cutlets with Creamy Herb Sauce p.46 + Fresh vegetables	1355
Day 3	Keto Pancakes with Butter and Syrup (2 servings) p.18	Keto Beef Stroganoff p.42 + Mushroom & Herb Cauliflower Rice p.59	Avocado Tuna Boats p.64	Creamy Garlic Mushroom Chicken p.37 + Leafy greens	1430
Day 4	Bacon and Avocado Caesar Salad p.27	Keto Eggplant Lasagna Roll-Ups p.58	Coconut Macaroons with Dark Chocolate (3 servings) p.70	Savory Stuffed Chicken Thighs with Mushrooms & Bacon p.40+Balsamic Roasted Vegetable Salad p.31	1435
Day 5	Zucchini and Almond Flour Breakfast Muffins (3 muffins) p.18	Garlic Butter Chicken Bites with Broccoli p.38	Coconut Lime Keto Bliss Balls (4 servings) p.74	Garlic Butter Shrimp with Keto Cauliflower Mash p.54	1315
Day 6	Crispy Bacon Egg and Cheese Roll-Ups p.13	Creamy Keto Egg & Salmon Salad p.34	Almond Butter Brownies (2 servings) p.71	Beef and Cabbage Stir-Fry p.47	1450
Day 7	Roasted Red Pepper and Egg Bake (1,5 servings) p.16	Keto Garlic Butter Squid with Roasted Bell Peppers p.52	Peanut Butter Fat Bombs (3 servings) p.69	Garlic-Parmesan Zucchini Noodle Salad (1,5 servings) p.59	1358
Day 8	Peanut Butter and Chocolate Keto Fat Bombs (2 servings) p.20	Creamy Cauliflower and Bacon Soup p.25	Pepperoni Chips with Ranch Dip (1,5 servings) p.61	Keto Pork Stir-Fry with Zucchini p.48	1370
Day 9	Smoked Salmon and Dill Egg Bites (3 egg bites) p.12	Keto Salmon Skewers with Roasted Zucchini p.53	Raspberry Almond Tarts (2 servings) p.70	Avocado & Shrimp Keto Caesar Salad p.33	1295
Day 10	Keto Pancakes with Butter and Syrup (2 servings) p.18	Spicy Sausage Kale Soup p.25	Low-Carb Ham and Cheese Roll-Ups (2 servings) p.67	Pork Tenderloin with Lemon Butter p.48 + 200 g. arugula	1570
Day 11	Pepperoni and Cheese Egg Cups p.14	Zucchini Noodles with Alfredo Sauce p.55	Keto Peanut Butter Blondies (2 servings) p.73	Keto Garlic Parmesan Shrimp Skewers (1,5 servings) p.65	1430
Day 12	Egg Salad-Stuffed Avocado Boats p.14	Keto Pork Stir-Fry with Zucchini p.48	Keto Chocolate Chip Cookies (3 servings) p.72	Keto Garlic Butter Squid with Roasted Bell Peppers p.52	1410
Day 13	Smoked Salmon and Dill Egg Bites (3 egg bites) p.12	Bacon Cheeseburger Casserole p.44 + Fresh vegetables	Avocado Tuna Boats p.64	Keto Beef Fajita Skillet p.46	1290
Day 14	Almond Butter and Coconut Yogurt Bowl p.17	Smoky Paprika Chicken Wings p.39 + Fresh leafy greens	Strawberry Cream Popsicles p.72	Thai Coconut Chicken Curry p.36 + Keto Faux Fried Rice with Egg p.57	1298
Day 15	Pepperoni and Cheese Egg Cups p.14	Creamy Cauliflower and Bacon Soup p.25	Almond Butter Brownies (2 servings) p.71	Keto Beef Fajita Skillet p.46	1400
Day 16	Lemon-Dill Salmon Salad p.29	Beef and Cabbage Stir-Fry p.47	Spicy Pork Rind Nachos p.63	Keto Pork Cutlets with Creamy Herb Sauce p.46 + Fresh vegetables	1425
Day 17	Smoked Salmon and Cucumber Breakfast Bites (2 servings) p.21	Creamy Garlic Mushroom Chicken p.37 + Leafy greens	Coconut Macaroons with Dark Chocolate (3 servings) p.70	Smoky Paprika Chicken Wings p.39 + Fresh leafy greens	1490
Day 18	Smoked Salmon and Dill Egg Bites (3 egg bites) p.12	Garlic Butter Shrimp with Keto Cauliflower Mash p.54	Keto Chocolate Chip Cookies (3 servings) p.72	Keto Salmon Skewers with Roasted Zucchini p.53	1315

Day	Breakfast	Lunch	Snack	Dinner	Kcal
Day 19	Spinach and Cheese Scrambled Egg Bowls (1,5 servings) p.15	Thighs with Mushrooms & Bacon p.40 + Fresh vegetables or greens	Raspberry Almond Tarts (2 servings) p.70	Bacon Cheeseburger Casserole p.44 + Fresh vegetables	1338
Day 20	Keto Pancakes with Butter and Syrup (2 servings) p.18	Avocado & Shrimp Keto Caesar Salad p.33	Chocolate Avocado Mousse p.69	Creamy Keto Egg & Salmon Salad p.34	1267
Day 21	Crispy Bacon Egg and Cheese Roll-Ups p.13	Thai Coconut Chicken Curry p.36	Peanut Butter Fat Bombs (3 servings) p.69	Smoky Paprika Chicken Wings p.39 + Fresh leafy greens	1490
Day 22	Zucchini and Almond Flour Breakfast Muffins (3 muffins) p.18	Keto Creamy Mussels with Sautéed Spinach p.54	Coconut Lime Keto Bliss Balls (4 servings) p.74	Keto Spicy Sriracha Salmon Steaks p.50 + Leafy greens	1305
Day 23	Smoked Salmon and Dill Egg Bites (3 egg bites) p.12	Creamy Broccoli Cheddar Soup p.23	Keto Peanut Butter Blondies (2 servings) p.73	Keto Garlic Parmesan Shrimp Skewers (1,5 servings) p.65	1385
Day 24	Peanut Butter and Chocolate Keto Fat Bombs (2 servings) p.20	Keto Eggplant Lasagna Roll-Ups p.58	Crispy Parmesan Chicken Nuggets (2 servings) p.63	Pork Tenderloin with Lemon Butter p.48 + 200 g. arugula	1390
Day 25	Creamy Keto Egg & Salmon Salad p.34	Balsamic Glazed Chicken Thighs p.39 + Warm Mushroom and Spinach Salad p.33	Low-Carb Ham and Cheese Roll-Ups (2 servings) p.67	Garlic Butter Shrimp with Keto Cauliflower Mash p.54	1550
Day 26	Pepperoni and Cheese Egg Cups p.14	Keto Korean Beef Bowls p.45 + Fresh vegetables	Keto Chocolate Chip Cookies (3 servings) p.72	Quick Keto Salmon Patties with Creamy Spinach p.52	1305
Day 27	Egg Salad-Stuffed Avocado Boats p.14	Keto Pork Stir-Fry with Zucchini p.48	Pepperoni Chips with Ranch Dip (1,5 servings) p.61	Keto Creamy Mussels with Sautéed Spinach p.54	1320
Day 28	Smoked Salmon and Dill Egg Bites (3 egg bites) p.12	Keto Taco Salad with Spiced Ground Beef p.31	Creamy Keto Coconut Panna Cotta p.73	Creamy Keto Egg & Salmon Salad p.34	1300
Day 29	Smoked Salmon and Cucumber Breakfast Bites (2 servings) p.21	Keto Chicken Alfredo Bake p.35 + Spicy Cabbage Slaw with Jalapeño p.30	Strawberry Cream Popsicles p.72	Keto Pork Cutlets with Creamy Herb Sauce p.46 + Fresh vegetables	1508
Day 30	Keto Pancakes with Butter and Syrup (2 servings) p.18	Spicy Sausage Kale Soup p.25	Coconut Macaroons with Dark Chocolate (3 servings) p.70	Crispy Sesame Chicken Tenders p.37	1410

Creating a Meal Plan for Your Keto Diet

Starting a keto diet can initially feel overwhelming, but creating a simple meal plan is a great way to stay on track. A meal plan helps you stay organized, avoid unnecessary temptation, and ensure you're meeting your nutritional needs while sticking to the five essential ingredients of the keto diet: healthy fats, protein, low-carb vegetables, dairy, and nuts/seeds.

Step 1: Plan for the Week

Begin by mapping out your meals for the week. Please keep it simple and focus on variety within the five key ingredients. A typical keto meal plan can include:
Breakfast, Lunch, Dinner and Snacks

Step 2: Replace Dishes When Needed

One of the best parts of a keto meal plan is flexibility. Swap ingredients or change cooking methods if you need more time to get bored with your usual meals. **For example:**

- If you're tired of eggs for breakfast, try a keto smoothie made with avocado, almond milk, and protein powder.
- For lunch, swap chicken for turkey or beef and change up the vegetable side dish, such as using cauliflower rice instead of leafy greens.
- For dinner, exchange salmon with another fatty fish or a cut of steak, keeping the healthy fats and protein balance.

Chopping List / 30 - Day

Chopping List / 1-7 day

Proteins:

- Beef sirloin - 100g
- Boneless, skinless chicken breasts - 450g
- Chicken breast - 100g
- Cooked ham - 100g
- Large eggs - 15
- Large skin-on, boneless chicken thighs - 150g
- Pepperoni slices - 30g
- Pork cutlets - 100g
- Pork loin, thinly sliced - 150g
- Rashers streaky bacon - 2
- Raw shrimp, peeled and deveined -125g
- Smoked salmon - 50g
- Squid, cleaned and sliced into rings - 50g
- Streaky bacon - 3 slices
- Tinned tuna in olive oil, drained - 40 g

Dairy:

- Cheddar cheese - 285g
- Crumbled feta cheese - 25g
- Double cream - 225ml
- Full-fat cream cheese - 15g
- Full-fat sour cream - 25g
- Grated mozzarella - 25g
- Heavy cream - 15ml
- Mozzarella balls - 50g
- Parmesan cheese - 65g
- Ricotta cheese - 50g

Fats:

- Almond butter - 50g
- Almond flour - 120g
- Avocado,large - 1
- Butter - 75g
- Coconut oil - 45g
- Mayonnaise - 45g
- Natural peanut butter (no added sugar) - 45g
- Olive oil
- Pesto - 10g
- Ripe avocados - 1
- Sesame oil - 15ml
- Unsalted butter - 50g

Vegetables and greens:

- Broccoli florets - 300g
- Cauliflower - 300g
- Cherry tomatoes - 25g
- Chestnut mushrooms - 25g
- Chopped chives - 30g
- Eggplant - 125g
- Fresh basil leaves - 2
- Fresh jalapeño, deseeded and finely chopped - Half
- Garlic - 6 cloves
- Large roasted red peppers (jarred or freshly roasted) - 2
- Leafy greens - 200g
- Mixed leafy greens - 25g
- Mushrooms - 150g
- Red bell pepper - 100g
- Romaine lettuce, chopped - 50g
- White cabbage, finely shredded - 100g
- Zucchini - 475g

Other Ingredients:

- Apple cider vinegar - 15ml
- Balsamic vinegar - 15ml
- Cesar dressing(check for low-carb options) - 30g
- Dark chocolate (85% cocoa or higher), melted - 25g
- Desiccated coconut - 85g
- Dijon mustard - 20g
- Lemon juice - 15ml
- Lime zest - - 15g
- Passata - 100ml
- Soy sauce (or tamari for gluten-free) - 15ml
- Sugar-free syrup - 15ml
- Unsweetened cocoa powder - 10g
- Usalted butter - 15g
- Wholegrain mustard - 15g

Spices:

- Baking powder - 10g
- Black pepper/ Sea salt
- Dried Italian herbs - 5g
- Dried oregano - 5g
- Dried parsley - 5g
- Powdered erythritol - 50g
- Smoked paprika - 15g
- Vanilla extract - 15g

Chopping List / 8-14 day

Proteins:

- Bacon, chopped - 25g
- Beef steak, sliced thinly - 150g
- Chicken breast, diced - 100g
- Chicken wings - 250g
- Cooked ham -100g
- Large egg - 13
- Minced beef - 100g
- Pepperoni slices - 70g
- Pork tenderloin - 450g
- Raw shrimp (peeled and deveined) - 325g
- Salmon fillet - 150g
- Smoked salmon - 75g
- Spicy sausage (e.g., chorizo)- 100g
- Squid, cleaned and sliced into rings - 125g
- Streaky bacon - 50g
- Tinned tuna in olive oil, drained - 40g

Dairy:

- Unsweetened coconut yogurt - 150g
- Cheddar cheese - 135g
- Cream cheese - 50g
- Double cream - 200g
- Parmesan cheese - 60g
- Greek yoghurt - 15g
- Sour cream - 40g

Fats:

- Almond butter -30g
- Almond flour - 150g
- Avocado - 100g
- Butter (plus extra for frying) - 15g
- Coconut milk - 50g
- Coconut oil - 8ml
- Mayonnaise - 40g
- Butter - 25g
- Natural peanut butter (no added sugar) - 100g
- Olive oil
- Ripe avocado - 2 pieces
- Sesame oil - 15ml
- Unsalted butter - 135g

Vegetables and greens:

- Arugula - 200g
- Bell pepper (Green) - Half
- Bell pepper (Red) - 1 piece
- Cauliflower - 300g
- Fresh dill, chopped - 15g
- Fresh leafy greens - 200g
- Fresh vegetables -200g
- Garlic - 3 clove
- Kale - 50g
- Spring onions - 1
- Zucchini - 425g

Other Ingredients:

- Baking powder
- Chia seeds - 15g
- Cocoa powder - 7g
- Desiccated coconut - 15g
- Dijon mustard - 15g
- Erythritol or preferred keto sweetener - 15g
- Fish sauce -5 ml
- Fresh raspberries - 30g
- Fresh strawberries - 25g
- Juice of 1 lemon
- Powdered erythritol - 50g
- Red curry paste - 5g
- Soy sauce (or tamari for gluten-free) - 40ml
- Sugar-free dark chocolate chips - 20g
- Sugar-free syrup - 15ml
- Tomato purée -10g
- Vanilla extract - 25 ml
- Wholegrain mustard - 15g

Spices:

- Black pepper
- Dried parsley
- Garlic powder
- Paprika
- Ried dill
- Sea salt
- Smoked paprika

Chopping List / 15-21 day

Proteins:

- Large skin-on, boneless chicken thighs - 150g
- Bacon, chopped - 25g
- Beef steak, sliced thinly - 150g
- Boneless, skinless chicken breasts - 150g
- Chicken breast - 100g
- Chicken wings - 500g
- Cooked salmon fillet, flaked - 100g
- Large egg - 16
- Minced beef - 250g
- Pepperoni slices - 30g
- Pork cutlets - 100g
- Pork rinds - 25g
- Raw shrimp, peeled and deveined - 225g
- Salmon fillet, cut into cubes - 150g
- Smoked salmon - 200g
- Streaky bacon, chopped - 80g

Dairy:

- Cheddar cheese - 120g
- Cream cheese - 75g
- Double cream - 210ml
- Feta cheese, crumbled - 40g
- Full-fat cream cheese - 15g
- Parmesan cheese, shaved - 2og
- Sour cream - 15ml

Fats:

- Olive oil - 8ml
- Almond butter - 50g
- Almond flour - 150g
- Butter - 40g
- Mayonnaise -40g
- Natural peanut butter (no added sugar) - 50g
- Ripe avocado - 175g
- Sesame oil - 8ml
- Unsalted butter - 75g

Vegetables and greens:

- Cauliflower florets - 300g
- Chestnut mushrooms - 25g
- Chopped chives - 1 bunch
- Cucumber - 150g
- Fresh dill, chopped - 35g
- Fresh leafy greens - 600g
- Fresh spinach - 75g
- Fresh vegetables - 600g
- Garlic - 2clove
- Green bell pepper - half
- Mushrooms - 50g
- Red bell pepper, sliced - half
- Shredded cabbage - 100g
- Sliced jalapeños - 8g
- Zucchini - 75g

Other Ingredients:

- Baking powder -
- Coconut milk - 50g
- Dark chocolate (85% cocoa or higher) - 25g
- Desiccated coconut - 50g
- Dijon mustard - 20g
- Fish sauce (15 ml) - 5ml
- Fresh raspberries - 30g
- Lemon juice - 5g
- Powdered erythritol - 80g
- Red curry paste (15g) - 5g
- Soy sauce (or tamari for gluten-free) - 15ml
- Sugar-free dark chocolate chips - 20g
- Sugar-free syrup - 15ml
- Tomato purée - 10g
- Unsweetened cocoa powder - 25g
- Vanilla extract - 15

Spices:

- Back pepper
- Dried parsley
- Garlic powder
- Ground ginger
- Paprika
- Salt and pepper
- Sea salt
- Smoked paprika

Chopping List / 22-30 day

Proteins:

- Boneless, skin-on chicken thighs -125g
- Canned salmon - 100g
- Chicken breast - 350g
- Cooked ham - 100g
- Ground beef (minced beef) - 100g
- Large eggs - 21
- Minced beef - 100g
- Mussels, cleaned - 500g
- Pepperoni slices - 80g
- Pork cutlets - 200g
- Pork loin - 150g
- Raw shrimp (peeled and deveined) - 375g
- Salmon steaks - 150g
- Smoked salmon - 275g
- Spicy sausage - 100g

Dairy:

- Cheddar cheese - 260g
- Cream cheese - 100g
- Double cream - 345ml
- Greek yoghurt - 15g
- Mozzarella - 25g
- Parmesan cheese - 40g
- Ricotta cheese - 50g
- Sour cream - 75g

Fats:

- Almond flour - 150g
- Avocado - half
- Butter - 45g
- Coconut oil
- Mayonnaise - 60g
- Natural peanut butter (no added sugar) - 100g
- Sesame oil - 15ml
- Unsalted butter - 50g

Spices:

- Dried dill
- Dried Italian herbs
- Dried parsley
- Dried thyme
- Garlic powder
- Ground cumin
- Paprika
- Sea salt
- Smoked paprika
- Vanilla extract

Vegetables and greens:

- Broccoli florets - 150g
- Cauliflower - 150g
- Chopped chives - 15g
- Cucumber - 100g
- Eggplant - 125g
- Fresh dill - 30g
- Fresh jalapeño - 1
- Fresh spinach - 150g
- Fresh vegetables - 400g
- Garlic - 5 cloves
- Kale- 50g
- Leafy greens - 250g
- Spring onions - 5g
- White cabbage - 100g
- Zucchini - 175g

Other Ingredients:

- Dark chocolate (85% cocoa or higher) - 25g
- Apple cider vinegar - 10ml
- Baking powder
- Balsamic vinegar - 15ml
- Cocoa powder - 10g
- Desiccated coconut - 85g
- Dijon mustard - 15g
- Fresh strawberries - 25g
- Full-fat coconut milk - 100ml
- Ginger - 2g
- Granulated erythritol - 5g
- Juice of 1 lime - 45ml
- Lime zest - 5g
- Passata - 100ml
- Powdered erythritol - 60g
- Powdered gelatin - 5g
- Sesame seeds - 10g
- Soy sauce (or tamari for gluten-free) - 15ml
- Sriracha sauce - 15ml
- Sugar-free syrup - 15ml
- Tamari (gluten-free soy sauce alternative) - 10ml
- Vanilla extract
- Wholegrain mustard - 15g

Conclusion: Your Journey to Simplified Keto Living

Congratulations on taking the first step toward making keto cooking simple, delicious, and approachable! With the recipes in The 5-Ingredient Keto Cookbook, you've unlocked the secret to creating flavorful, nutritious meals without the stress of complicated ingredients or hours in the kitchen.

By now, you've seen how easy it is to enjoy a variety of keto-friendly dishes that align with your goals, whether it's weight loss, boosting energy, or simply embracing a healthier lifestyle. These recipes were designed to prove that simplicity can be both satisfying and sustainable, even on a ketogenic diet.

Thank you for purchasing this book and allowing me to join your keto journey. Your commitment to health and wellness is truly inspiring, and I hope these recipes become staples in your kitchen.

As a special thank you, remember to claim your exclusive bonus content by scanning the QR code provided in the book. This bonus includes additional resources, tips, and recipes to keep your keto adventure fresh and exciting.

BONUS 1 / Keto Vegan Recipes

BONUS 2 / Keto Bread Resipes

BONUS 3 / Keto Smoothie Recipes

If you've enjoyed this cookbook, I'd be incredibly grateful if you could share your feedback in a review. Your support helps others discover how easy and enjoyable keto living can be.

Here's to your continued success and delicious meals ahead!

MEASUREMENT CONVERSION TABLES

VOLUME EQUIVALENTS (LIQUID)

STANDART	STANDART (OUNCES)	METRIC (APPROXIMATE)
2 tablespoons	1 fl.oz.	30 ml
¼ cup	2 fl.oz.	60 ml
½ cup	4 fl.oz.	120 ml
1 cup	8 fl.oz.	240 ml
1½ cups	12 fl.oz.	355 ml
2 cups or 1 pint	16 fl.oz.	475 ml
4 cups or 1 quart	32 fl.oz.	1 L
1 gallon	128 fl.oz.	4 L

OVEN TEMPERATURES

FAHRENHEIT (F)	CELSIUS (C) (APPROXIMATE)
250°F	120°C
300°F	150°C
325°F	165°C
350°F	180°C
375°F	190°C
400°F	200°C
425°F	220°C
450°F	230°C

VOLUME EQUIVALENTS (DRY)

STANDART	STANDART (OUNCES)
¼ teaspoon	1 ml
½ teaspoon	2 ml
1 teaspoon	5 ml
1 tablespoon	15 ml
¼ cup	59 ml
⅓ cup	79 ml
½ cup	118 ml
1 cup	235 ml

WEIGHT EQUIVALENTS

STANDART	METRIC (APPROXIMATE)
½ ounce	15g
1 ounce	30g
2 ounces	60g
4 ounces	115g
8 ounces	225g
12 ounces	340g
16 ounces or 1 pound	455g

Printed in Great Britain
by Amazon

59726996R00051